CO-021

A COMPLETE INTRODUCTION TO
MARINE AQUARIUMS

An adult Queen Angelfish (Holacanthus ciliaris). Juvenile Queen Angels are commonly kept by marine aquarists.

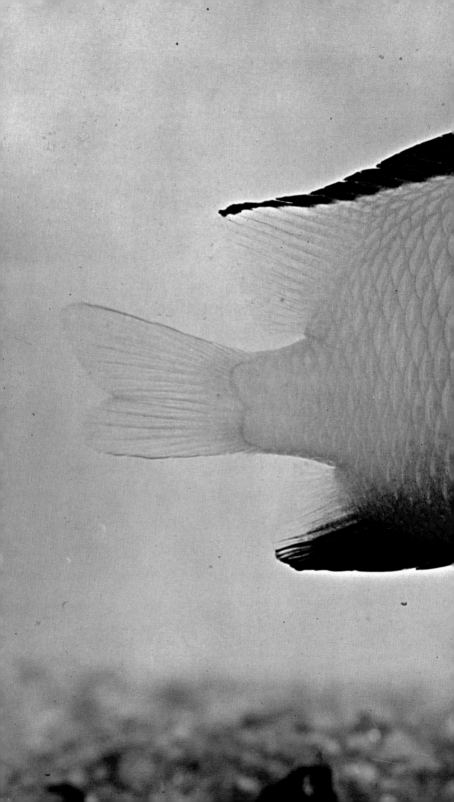

One of the more popular species of Dascyllus from the Red Sea area is this D. marginatus.

A COMPLETE INTRODUCTION TO

MARINE AQUARIUMS

COMPLETELY ILLUSTRATED IN FULL COLOR

The Pacific Blue Tang (Paracanthurus hepatus) is strikingly patterned and colored.

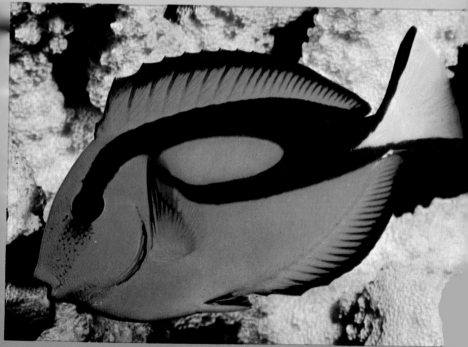

Dr. Warren E. Burgess

Photography

We are indebted to the following photographers without whose fine work this book wouldn't have been possible.

Allen, Dr. Gerald R.
Axelrod, Dr. Herbert R.
Bertschy, A. (courtesy Dr. D. Terver)
Burgess, Dr. Warren E.
Choo, Kok-Hang, Teipei Aquarium
Colin, Dr. Patrick L.
Courtesy of L'Arche de Noe
Deas, Walter
Faulkner, Douglas
Frickhinger, K. A.
Gillet, Keith
Goto, Michio, Marine Life Documents
Gray, Noel
Hansen, H., Aquarium Berlin
Johnson, Scott
Kahl, B.
Kennedy, Earl
Kerstitch, Alex
Lomas, J. A.,

Lucas, Ken, Steinhart Aquarium
Marine Studios, Marineland, Florida
Moyer, Dr. Jack T.
Nigrelli, Dr. F. R., Osborne Labs.
Norman, Aaron
Peter, Hans
Power, Allan
Probst, Karl
Randall, Dr. John E.
Reichenbach-Klinke, Dr. H.
Ruggieri, G. D., Osborne Labs
Smith, George
Steene, Roger
Straughan, Robert P. L.
Suzuki, K.
Takemura, Y.
Teh, Anthony
Terver, Dr. D., Nancy Aquarium
van den Nieuwenhuizen, Arend
Yasuda, Dr. Fujio

This book is dedicated to Mr. Murray Wiener who has taught me a great deal about marine fishes and how to maintain them.

Distributed in the UNITED STATES by T.F.H. Publications, Inc., 211 West Sylvania Avenue, Neptune City, NJ 07753; in CANADA to the Pet Trade by H & L Pet Supplies Inc., 27 Kingston Crescent, Kitchener, Ontario N2B 2T6; Rolf C. Hagen Ltd., 3225 Sartelon Street, Montreal 382 Quebec; in CANADA to the Book Trade by Macmillan of Canada (A Division of Canada Publishing Corporation), 164 Commander Boulevard, Agincourt, Ontario M1S 3C7; in ENGLAND by T.F.H. Publications Limited, 4 Kier Park, Ascot, Berkshire SL5 7DS; in AUSTRALIA AND THE SOUTH PACIFIC by T.F.H. (Australia) Pty. Ltd., Box 149, Brookvale 2100 N.S.W., Australia; in NEW ZEALAND by Ross Haines & Son, Ltd., 18 Monmouth Street, Grey Lynn, Auckland 2 New Zealand; in SINGAPORE AND MALAYSIA by MPH Distributors (S) Pte., Ltd., 601 Sims Drive, #03/07/21, Singapore 1438; in the PHILIPPINES by Bio-Research, 5 Lippay Street, San Lorenzo Village, Makati Rizal; in SOUTH AFRICA by Multipet Pty. Ltd., 30 Turners Avenue, Durban 4001. Published by T.F.H. Publications Inc. Manufactured in the United States of America by T.F.H. Publications, Inc.

CONTENTS

Introduction

The marine aquarium is really not very hard to set up, you know. It used to be, but no longer. Among the items that have caused this change is, first of all, the all-glass tank. This has eliminated the problem of metal contamination of your water with the ensuing demise of your prized specimens. Secondly, artificial salts have come a long way from the time when it was much safer to travel many miles to collect your own sea water than to depend on some of the concoctions available on the market. Now we are also even paying attention to trace elements. But perhaps the real breakthrough was not a physical item as such, but a theory, one that showed us what we were doing wrong and what we should do to make it work. This was the theory of biological filtration. How many early marine aquarists ever heard of the nitrogen cycle? Or knew the deadly effects of ammonia or nitrites? How many wondered why their fishes died in such sparkling clean newly set up aquaria? Or why fishes seemed to die soon after the filter was thoroughly

A large marine aquarium can be decorated with various corals and house an assortment of fishes. Here tangs, wrasses, butterflyfishes, and an angelfish are doing very well.

cleaned? Now we know. Armed with this knowledge and the paraphernalia available to us at the nearest pet shop, we are able to approach the setting up of a marine aquarium with a high probability for success. Those fishes you have been ogling at your marine aquarium store are within reach. Just by keeping your wits about you and following carefully the instructions and advice currently available to you, those breathtaking fishes can soon be in your own marine tank providing you with countless hours of fishwatching pleasure. Who knows—perhaps in a very short time you will be attempting, and succeeding, at spawning some of the easier species. After that, bring on those difficult species!

Basic Equipment

The first item that a budding marine aquarist must consider is the tank. Everything else revolves around this one main piece of equipment. All the accessories must be compatible with the tank, they must operate the tank at peak efficiency, the positioning and supporting structures must fit the tank, and the fishes you probably have in mind for the tank must be able to live happily in it.

Of course it must be an all-glass tank. Perhaps experienced aquarists can get away with other types of tanks, but if you look around it seems even the experts have all switched to the all-glass tank. And why not—it's so much easier and safer. They are quite inexpensive, they are dependable, and even if you wanted some other type it may prove difficult to even find one. How long has it been since you went into a reliable aquarium store and saw anything other than all-glass tanks—for both freshwater and marine fishes?

Acrylic tanks seem to be making a comeback. They have both advantages and disadvantages when compared to all-glass tanks. First of all they are often one-piece construction, making them unlikely to split a seam like some all-glass tanks. Secondly, they are much lighter than similar sized all-glass tanks. On the drawback side they are more expensive, they are prone to scratching (this is being worked on) and they may yellow with age (although some of the newer tanks may not).

The size of the tank is of utmost importance. The bigger the better. I would

All-glass tanks have changed the marine aquarium hobby considerably. They make marine fish keeping almost easy.

recommend a 55-gallon tank as a good starter. It's big enough to buffer some of the mistakes you are bound to make and big enough to house a reasonable assortment of fishes—at least enough to keep you happy for a while. But of course many novice marine aquarists are hesitant to start with such a seemingly large undertaking, so they opt for something more "manageable," say a 20- or 30-gallon tank. This can be done, but it is quite a bit harder than with the bigger tank. Such hesitant beginners argue that when you get reasonably proficient with the smaller tank, the larger one will appear that much easier, and you can use the smaller tank as your quarantine or utility tank when you switch to the bigger one. Who can argue with that logic?

You can purchase a ready-made tank or you can build one yourself. Considering the prices of the ready-made item, it is much more economical to buy one of these and only build your own if there is a real necessity to do so, such as if you wanted to build it into a space where standard sizes would not fit or if for some reason you wanted an oddly shaped aquarium (although even ready-made aquaria come in an assortment of shapes as well as sizes). There are a variety of ready-made aquaria available, ranging from the rather simple ones to those with simulated wood grain

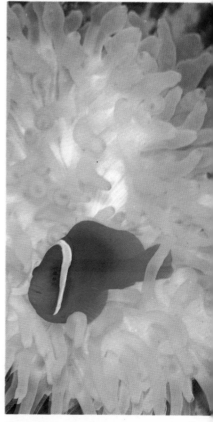

Clownfishes are often the first fishes kept. This is Amphiprion frenatus in an anemone.

finishes that are quite pleasing to the eye. Many of the tanks even come with guarantees.

Once the tank has been selected, everything else starts to fall into place. The support or stand must be considered next. Since salt water weighs in the neighborhood of 8½ pounds per gallon, you can figure how much support is needed. Remember to include the weight of the tank itself, the gravel, decorations, and whatever else is in or on the tank. Aquarium stands of all sorts, from simple metal rod types to those covered in elegant wood grain, are available. For a showpiece in your living room the latter seems more appropriate. The ultimate choice is up to you.

During this time you must have had a site for the aquarium already in mind. You were careful to have it near electrical outlets from which to run the various necessities of the tank. It is not an area where cold drafts or extreme heat would affect the tank, such as next to a radiator or an air conditioner. A certain amount of light from a window may be beneficial to a tank; after all, most of the fishes you select will be from well-lighted coral reef areas, but too much light will cause an overgrowth of algae and in the summer perhaps an undesirable heating effect. It is usually best to be in firm control of all aspects of your aquarium. The tank must also be in a favorable viewing position, perhaps at eye level

Aquaria built into a wall give the effect of a "living picture." Be sure sufficient access for feeding and maintenance are available.

when you are sitting down and relaxing in your favorite comfortable chair.

I hope I do not have to remind you that there is a possibility of splashes (water changes and startled fishes are but two sources) and that anything that is not supposed to get wet (stereos, books, etc.) should be a safe distance away. Room must also be provided for the various accessories that are needed—pumps, filters, and the like.

Perhaps filters and pumps are the next items to take under consideration. With the equipment available today pumps and filters usually mean only a single item, that being the power filter. The variety of these power filters can be dazzling. There are, however, three basic types that can be used individually or even in combination with one another. First of all there is the canister filter. This is a canister that contains the filtering material and has a pump sitting on top of it to propel the water back into the tank after it has been filtered. The water enters the filter by gravity. The return water is usually sprayed back into the

Above right: *This round tank serves as a base for a small bar top. Care must be taken no overly heavy objects are set on top.* **Below right:** *Avid marine aquarists even find space in the kitchen for a tank.*

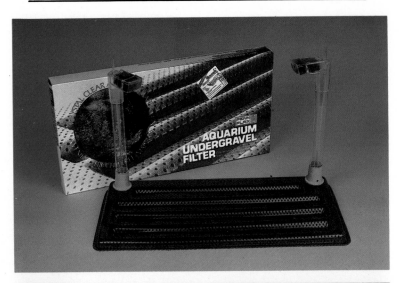

tank so that it is aerated. A second combination is a box containing the filtering material that hangs on the side of the tank and is provided with a motor that drives the water through it. The filtered water is also sometimes returned to the tank with an aerating effect. The third major type is the undergravel filter. The filter

Two types of filtering system, the undergravel filter (above) and the outside power filter (below). Each has its advocates and some aquarists even use both together.

All three types of filters do their job. How well they do it depends a lot on the aquarist. With an aquarist who tends to overfeed or to "forget" about the water changes every so often, there is a need for a filtration system more powerful than that normally necessary for a more careful feeder or dedicated water changer. Look over the different systems at your aquarium store and select the one that you feel comfortable with.

Heaters are needed if the temperature of the water is to be maintained above the ambient room temperature. They are almost all now fitted with thermostats to keep the

The third type filter is the canister filter seen here. They come in different sizes for different capacity tanks.

sits in the tank under the gravel (often with a mat of filtering material between the gravel and filter); the water is drawn out from below the filter, thus forcing it to pass through the gravel, etc., to provide the filtering action, and is returned to the tank at the surface of the water. A separate pump is usually needed for the undergravel filter although there are power-operated undergravel filters available.

A good quality heater is necessary if the temperature is to be maintained above the ambient room temperature.

Basic Equipment

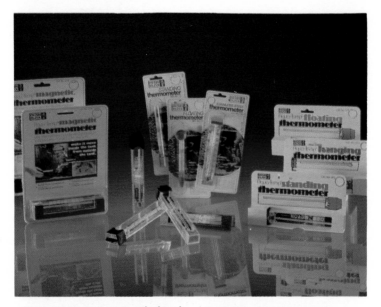

temperature at a certain level. Most work very well. Heaters come in different wattages to handle different heating situations, so select the one that is designed to work with the size tank that has been selected. Since heater failures can be disastrous, be sure to select a reliable one even if it costs an extra dollar or two. A thermometer in or on the tank is also necessary in order to check the efficiency of the heater. I find the digital strip best since it is easily readable and can be checked relatively often.

The light and cover usually come as a single unit and shall be covered together here. Often there is a glass or plastic partition between the light and tank, protecting the light and other parts of the hood from the spray of the water. Even if the spray is under control, condensation

A variety of thermometers are available. Choose one that suits your needs best. Make sure there are no metal parts that can come into contact with the water.

would otherwise collect on the light and electrical connections, usually causing problems, possibly even dangerous ones.

The tank cover also helps keep evaporation to a minimum. An uncovered heated tank seems to need topping off quite often, whereas one that is covered retains the moisture in the tank much longer. Another reason for the hood or cover is to keep your fishes in the tank. It's a fact of life that fishes jump, and it seems they almost always decide to leave the tank by this method during the middle of the night

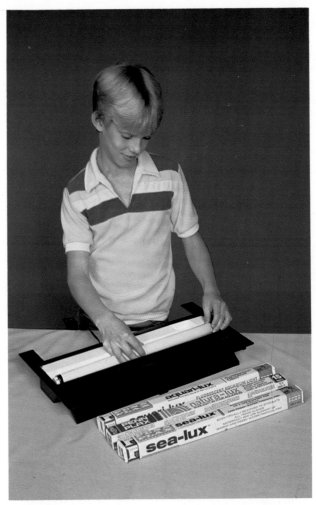

Fluorescent bulbs for specific purposes can be purchased at your dealer's shop.

much more prevalent. Fluorescent bulbs come in a variety of wavelengths for special purposes. This is a boon to aquarists who want luxuriant algal growths for their fishes to feed upon. They simply select the proper bulb for plant growth and plug it in. Other bulbs give off light that is particularly flattering to the fishes. Many dealers use these bulbs to show their fishes off to the best

and not when you are available to rescue them.

Lights come with either incandescent or fluorescent bulbs, the latter becoming

advantage for their customers. Fluorescent lights are more economical to operate, which is a consideration for some energy-conscious people, especially since they are usually on for 12 hours a day.

Although ultraviolet light sterilization has been around for many years, it had not really been considered as a real necessity for marine aquarists. Recently, however, it has been getting more and more attention. Basically, the unit is an ultraviolet lamp housed in a protective envelope in a way that water can be pumped through the envelope so that the ultraviolet rays can kill the harmful organisms before the water is returned to the tank. Since ultraviolet light is harmful to both fishes and man, care must be exercised when using one. However, newer units are on the market that are quite safe when used as directed. Perhaps this is the wave of the future. One

Ultraviolet sterilizers are becoming more popular with marine aquarists. New ones are better constructed than those previously available.

objection was raised concerning ultraviolet sterilizers. Wouldn't it kill the "good" bacteria along with the "bad" ones? The answer is yes, if the "good" bacteria left their biological filter to be carried through the sterilizer. But most of them don't, so they remain quite safe doing their important jobs. (Biological filtration will be discussed later on.) The ultraviolet bulb lasts about six to eight months before it needs to be replaced. One word of advice: never use the sterilizer on a medicated tank—it may change the chemical structure of the medication.

Ozonizers remove dissolved organic material as well as kill bacteria and parasites. They therefore do much the same job as the ultraviolet sterilizer. Yet ozonizers are said to still be delicate instruments and perhaps even dangerous, so they are not yet recommended.

Protein skimmers remove large organic molecules such as proteins, fatty acids, and amino acids, as well as certain dyes, detergents, etc. As such they are a useful tool, but they take some time and trouble to get operating correctly. Skimmers are hard to adjust for maximum efficiency.

Ion exchange resins are still poorly known and perhaps best left on the shelf until they are more thoroughly researched.

Test equipment is quite important in a marine aquarium. Aside from the usual pH kit and nitrate-nitrite-ammonia kits, a marine aquarist needs some way in which to test the salinity of the water. This is easily done by means of a hydrometer. This instrument in its most basic form is a tubular glass envelope, thicker on the bottom, that is weighted in such a way that when floated in water it will sink a specific distance depending upon the amount of salts in the water. It is relatively easy then to construct a scale of values and place the scale in such a way that the specific gravity can be read directly at the water's surface. In addition to the hydrometer, more elaborate chemical and electronic test kits are available giving more accurate readings of not only the specific gravity but the salinity

Copper can be tested for with the special kits available.

19

as well (salinity can be obtained from specific gravity and temperature readings by means of a chart).

The pH for sea water is determined in much the same way as that of fresh water except that marine water has

a higher (more alkaline) pH than most fresh waters (with the exception of some of the water suitable for Rift Lake cichlids) and is read off different scales. When you buy a pH test kit be sure it specifically says that it is for marine aquaria.

The ammonia-nitrite-nitrate test kits work like some of the pH kits. The values are determined by adding specific chemicals to the test water and comparing the color of the resulting solution to color charts. This type of test kit is quite important as you can monitor the development of your biological filter when you first set up your tank and you can keep track of potential problems by watching the values for ammonia and nitrites.

The substrate you select for a marine tank often has a chemical role to play. Beside

Test kits for measuring the pH, ammonia and nitrite levels, hardness, etc. are available as individual kits (above and below) or they may be combined into a complete analysis package that deals with everything.

being something to cover the bare bottom of the tank (assuming an undergravel filter is not used) and support decorations and plants as it does in a freshwater tank, it helps buffer the pH. Dolomite, crushed coral rock, and similar materials are basically calcium carbonate and as such tend to keep the pH of the water from drifting toward the acid side. This same material can be used for

Almost every marine tank is decorated with coral. The red organ-pipe coral gives some color to the tank.

similar reasons in your Rift Lake cichlid tank.

Decorations for a marine tank are more limited than those for freshwater aquaria. For a marine tank coral skeletons that have been carefully cleaned are the most desirable. They immediately identify the tank as marine and give it a more natural look. Most are very attractive. Since they are composed of calcium carbonate, they also help with the pH buffering.

Recently artificial decorations for marine aquaria have become available. These include not

only simulated corals but also artificial marine plants for those who simply must have plants in the aquarium. Since beauty is in the eye of the beholder, the selection of the decorations is up to the aquarist.

If possible—and this is often difficult—suit the decorations to the fishes or other animals you expect to house in the tank. Some fishes, such as cardinalfishes and squirrelfishes, are nocturnal and need some darkish caves or similar regions where they can hide during the day; others need plenty of open water for swimming, and such space should therefore be provided.

There are other accessories available, but the ones listed above are those that you are most likely to encounter or need while you are learning how to operate a marine tank. Some of them can be used in both marine and freshwater tanks, while others are specifically designed for the marine tank. Be sure you know which ones you need when you are purchasing your equipment.

For those aquarists that prefer a natural looking background there are photographic representations available to fit the size tank you have selected.

The Marine Water

The basic difference between marine and freshwater aquaria is, of course, the water itself. Salt water is a very complex and dynamic fluid containing, among other things, chemicals not found in fresh water, at least not in the same proportions or quantities. Those chemicals that make the difference are very important to the marine fishes, and lack of certain ones, even if they are found in salt water in the minutest amounts, can sometimes make the difference between

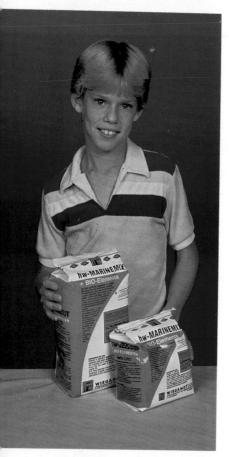

life and death for them. At first natural sea water was the only way to supply marine fishes with what they needed. The artificial salts seemed to be lacking in something, and the deficiency showed up by distress in the fishes, if not right away then within a few weeks or months of their addition to the tank. But the chemists got busy and came up with workable formulas so that now there are several excellent packaged salts that, when mixed with fresh water, produce an aquatic environment that the fishes are happy with. At least they do not die as they used to. Some seem not to notice the difference at all, even to the extent that they will spawn in the artificial sea water.

But what happens when the inhabitants of a tank use up some of these critical materials? Well, there are two ways in which they are replenished. First, there are packaged trace elements available at your aquarium store. What could be simpler than to add these trace elements periodically as they become used up? Secondly, a system of water changes like those done for freshwater tanks should also be set up for a marine aquarium. The water changes not only help

Marine mixes are much more reliable today than they were in the early marine hobbyist days and there is a reasonable selection to choose from.

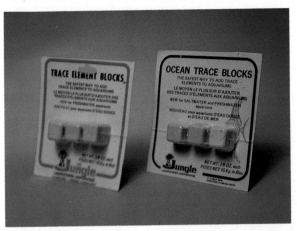

As trace elements are used up in a marine tank they can be replaced periodically by use of these blocks.

in replacing some of the trace elements, but they rid the tank of a portion of the unwanted materials that naturally build up in a closed system.

What brand of artificial salts should you get? Check with your dealer. He should know which one best works with your local water supply.

If you insist on collecting your own sea water, be sure to get it from an unpolluted source. Even when I lived in Miami, I would spurn the inshore water and fill up several 5-gallon carboys with pure Gulf Stream water from a mile or so offshore. Once collected, the natural water should be filtered. After all, there are animals and plants living in it even though you cannot see them without the aid of a microscope. Then store the water in the dark for two to three weeks and filter it again (with a diatom filter if you have one) before using it.

When dealing with marine fishes remember that they are living in a limited amount of water in your aquarium. Where they came from, however, the water was to all intents and purposes unlimited. It is your job to reduce the difference between these two environments to the absolute minimum within your abilities. The better you succeed the more your fishes will show their appreciation by longer lives, brighter colors, greater normal activity, and perhaps even a spawning or two. To do this you must pay careful attention to the water quality—the composition, the trace elements, the specific gravity, the oxygen and carbon dioxide content, and especially the amounts of dangerous pollutants.

Setting Up

Setting up a marine aquarium is not much more difficult than setting up a freshwater tank. First of all, the stand should be placed where you want the aquarium to be. Remember that once the tank is set up it is a lot of work to change its position. It may be a good idea to place an expendable but presentable piece of carpet or other the exuberance of a fish to snatch a morsel of food when you drop it into the tank, or the time when you reach into a tank and your arm comes out dripping wet. That's just a fact of life. I have used this method with great success. The section of carpet can eventually be changed when the tank is drained for one reason or another.

material beneath the stand in order to protect your carpet or floor or other substrate on which the tank stands from dripping seawater. And don't just say you will be careful. Of course you will, but there will always be the "accident" such as a sudden movement by a fish as you startle it when you are making a water change,

A suitable support for the selected aquarium should be purchased or constructed. A commercialy available stand should fit the basic tank sizes perfectly.

The stand is placed in position and the tank carefully seated on top of it. Make sure the tank rests solidly and evenly on its support or unwanted stresses may eventually take their toll. Some aquarists place a mat of some sort (a half inch of styrofoam seems to be popular for this) on top of the stand beneath the tank to "fill in" the uneven places. With tank and stand in position it is up to you to select in which sequence you want to add everything else. If you are using an undergravel filter, that goes in first with a thin mat of filter floss or similar material on top of it. The idea behind the filter floss is to help prevent the substrate (dolomite, crushed coral, or similar substances) from clogging the filter slots as well as to provide some filtering action. The dolomite goes on top of this in the normal manner.

Without the undergravel filter I prefer to place the dolomite in first. By placing the dolomite in first you don't have to work around any of the equipment, possibly knocking it off the tank and damaging some of it. Since the dolomite is generally wet (I'll get to that), putting it in first leaves less opportunity for any of it to foul up items that should remain dry and free from pieces of dolomite or grit. Anyway, the dolomite, crushed coral gravel, or whatever material you have selected should first be washed just like the sand or gravel you might place in a freshwater tank. Even

If no undergravel filter is used the washed bottom material (dolomite) can be added first.

prewashed material should be rinsed since the pieces rubbing against each other create some grit no matter how careful you are. You can see from the first bucketful (using a bucket and hose is one of the easiest methods of washing the dolomite) how much rinsing or washing is needed. Usually after directing a strong flow of water into the dolomite and then stopping it and waiting a few seconds you will see whether the water is clear or not. If it is, carefully pour the fresh water out and place the dolomite in the tank. Then rinse the next bucketful, and so on. With all the dolomite in the tank you can grade it so that the deeper portions are at the back. This allows gravity to help you collect much of the detritus in the front of the tank, where it is relatively easy to reach when you siphon the bottom. Although this sounds great in theory, it works only on a limited scale since decorations get in the way and certain fishes seem to like to redecorate the aquarium by shifting the substrate around to their liking.

The decorations should be positioned next. It is much easier to place them in an empty tank than it is to try and set them up underwater. In fact, some aquarists prefer to place the decorations in the tank before adding the substrate. This provides the decorations with a firmer base in case some of those dolomite-moving fishes undermine them. If you decide to add the decorations after the dolomite is in place, it is a simple matter to push or wiggle them down into the substrate until they rest firmly on the tank bottom. That way you do not have to try and place the dolomite around the decorations.

The coral pieces that are generally used for decorations can be set up in whatever pattern you wish. There are a few things you might remember, however. You want to be able to view your fishes, so do not place large pieces near the front. You also want to provide hiding places for the shy or nocturnal species. This may sound counterproductive, but you will find that when the fishes feel secure they are more apt to be out in the open more often knowing that they

are only a fraction of a second away from shelter. Place the decorations in such a way that it will be easy to clean around them and to inspect areas where detritus may accumulate. This is the time to make easier on yourself the chores that must be done later when the tank is full of water. When you are satisfied with the decor, step back and take a good look at it. Even if it looks great, review the maintenance chores you will be performing. Netting out fishes has to be done from time to time. Will the net get caught in the coral? Can you even hope to catch the fish without tearing the tank apart? Can you remove selected pieces of coral without destroying the rest of the tank? Can you clean the front glass without anything getting in the way? I'm sure you might think of some more potential problems, but you get the idea. If you are in no hurry, maybe you can take a break and then return for another look before continuing in case something has escaped your notice.

The placement of the pump and filter combination can be next. It is always a good idea to get all the tubing in place before adding other

The coral decorations can then be added making sure they are solidly resting on the tank bottom and will not fall if undermined by digging fishes.

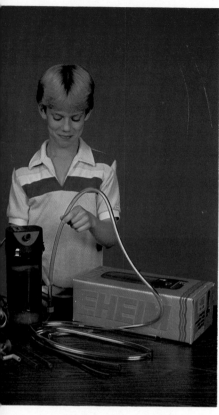

The filters can be set up according to the manufacturer's instructions. The critical part is to get the proper lengths and orientation of the plastic tubing.

assortment of substances. Dolomite has been used with success as it adds more pH buffering material to the system. Activated carbon removes dissolved organic matter; it is best used in outside power filters. The activity of the carbon may last up to a year before it must be changed. It may be best to use less carbon but change it more often, say about every month, to be sure to obtain full advantage of its properties. It also should be used sparingly just after water changes or when there are invertebrates in the tank. It should never be used in a tank that has been medicated as it will remove the medication, rendering the treatment useless. Filter floss also is used, often in combination with one or more of the other substances.

Again step back and review the arrangement. Will everything operate as it is now laid out? If so, on to the next step.

Okay, now add the heater. The position depends on several things. Will it be visible from the front even if it is not supposed to be? Can the thermostat be adjusted easily? Will it fit into one of the openings so provided in the hood? Do not forget the

accessories. It is often difficult to work it around heaters and the like. Remember that the cover or hood will go on top, so provision for exit of tubing must be made. Some hood/light combinations make allowance for these things by providing cut-outs for them. You may also find that the filter intakes are interfered with by the decorations and some rearranging must be done.

The filter material can be added and the filter set up as per instructions of the manfacturer. The filter material can be an

With the heater in place you can now position the thermometer. You do not want it directly next to the heater but normally should place it at the opposite end of the tank. Some aquarists like to pre-test their heaters in smaller containers so that the thermostat is set at the proper temperature when it is ready for the big tank. This is of course optional since you will have time to do this *in situ* before fishes are ever added.

A digital thermometer is easy to read from a distance and can be checked quickly to see if the heater is functioning properly.

The heater should be positioned for maximum efficiency. It must also be placed with an eye toward the hood that will fit over it.

circulation pattern of the tank: the filter will be causing currents in the tank, so you want the heater to be as well positioned as possible to take advantage of this and circulate the heat in the most efficient manner. You also do not want the splash or spray from the filter or airstones (if used) to strike the upper part of the heater.

31

Airstones, if used, can now be added. This normally means an additional pump if the filtering system is of the power type. With proper filtration airstones are not needed, as the filter provides sufficient aeration by its actions, but it may be good to have some means of aeration as a back-up system for those times when the filter is torn down for cleaning. For those aquarists in areas where there are numerous power outages, it might be a good idea even to invest in a battery operated pump. This could help your fishes over difficult times.

Optional equipment may be added whenever it seems advisable to you. Only you know how many accessories are to be added and where they will best fit. Things like ultraviolet sterilizers should be placed fairly early, external decorative items fairly late. The light and hood should go on last, after the water has been added, but only after it has been fitted in place over the dry tank to see if everything fits where it should. If the light and hood combination does not have a plastic or glass partition between it and the tank it is advisable to get one. These are also available at your aquarium store. This partition

A large piece of Acropora coral. The selection of the decorations depends upon your artistic leanings.

Setting Up

Two popular marine fishes, Zanclus canescens *(above) and* Pterois volitans *(below).*

Once you have selected the particular salt mix that will provide you with salt water, you should read the instructions carefully. Not all mixes are prepared the same way and you do not want to make mistakes at this point. It is usually best if you can make your salt water in a separate container and add it to the newly set up aquarium when you are ready for it. Some manufacturers of sea salt recommend that their product mature for a period of time (usually 24 hours) under aeration or in the dark, or both. Water mixed in a separate container is also easier to adjust if the salinity (density) or pH is not quite right, although you will have another opportunity when the biological filter is maturing. When the mixing is completed you can check the specific gravity and pH of the water and make adjustments as needed.

The water you use for mixing should be relatively free from contaminants. Even the tap water that you drink might cause problems if it contains chloramines. Your dealer can probably advise you on how safe your water is and what to do if it is not safe. There are commercial preparations that will remove chlorine and chloramines rather easily.

protects the workings of the light from the salt water.

With everything in place you should again step back and contemplate what you have done. This is especially important now since this is your last chance to change anything while the tank is dry, for the next step is to add the water.

When the water is ready you can start adding it to your aquarium. Don't just pour it in by the bucketful, for you will certainly undo all the effort you spent decorating the tank. The water can be siphoned in if you are willing to take the time, but if you are in a hurry you can probably get away with the least damage by carefully pouring the water onto one of the coral pieces that will not move when the water hits it. As the tank fills up you can pour a little faster, as the water itself absorbs some of the shock. Pouring the water onto a floating piece of styrofoam or plastic may be tried with good results.

When you have filled the tank to the proper level—a level where your equipment will operate correctly—you may notice that you have some water left over even though you mixed 30 gallons of water for a 30-gallon tank. Part of this is due to the fact that you do not fill the tank completely but only to within an inch or so of the top, and part is due to the volume of the decorations, etc., that are now in the tank. The volume of water left over should approximately equal the volume of the decorations added. Remember also that the stated volumes of tanks are conventions, not true measurements; a 30-gallon tank may hold only 27 gallons, for instance. The extra water may be stored and used for the first water change.

You can now start some of

Pouring water into a tank should be done carefully. A dish can be used as shown to prevent scattering of the substrate material.

the equipment operating— filters, airstones, heaters— and make additional adjustments as needed. The temperature should be adjusted to approximately 75-82°F (24-28°C), the specific gravity to 1.020-1.026 (28-35 ppt), and the pH to 7.8-8.1.

Although the tank now looks beautiful even without fishes, you must be patient and start setting up the biological filter.

Biological Filtration

To properly "age" an aquarium, whether it is a marine or a freshwater aquarium, you have to get a biological filter operating. A biological filter is approximately what the name says—a filter that depends not on mechanical or chemical means to rid the tank of unwanted substances, but upon living organisms to do the work. Since these living organisms are bacteria and they are intimately involved in a biological cycle involving nitrogen as one of the main constituents, it is therefore called the nitrogen cycle. Although it is not absolutely essential that you understand the operation of the nitrogen cycle, it does help you understand why you are doing what you are doing. It also may help you prevent or fix something going wrong with the cycle.

Fishes and other animals in the aquarium excrete a variety of organic compounds, as well as ammonia, a substance that is deadly to the animals themselves in high enough concentrations. In addition, uneaten food and dead fishes that are decomposing also produce harmful organic compounds and ammonia. This process is called ammonification. Some of these harmful substances can be removed by careful aquarium cleaning and water changes; others are sucked up by the filter and must be handled there since they are still within the aquarium system. Luckily for the aquarist, there are bacteria of the genus *Nitrosomonas* that chemically convert the deadly ammonia to another nitrogen compound called a nitrite. Although not as deadly as the ammonia, nitrites are still lethal in high enough concentrations. It was probably high levels of ammonia and nitrites that killed off a large number of fishes in the early days of marine aquarium keeping. If we had only known!

The problem of the nitrites still remains. However, other beneficial organisms, bacteria of the genus *Nitrobacter*, come to the aid of the aquarist. These helpful

With the discovery of the processes of biological filtration manufacturers rushed to develop products aquarists would need.

bacteria convert the nitrites to nitrates, a relatively harmless substance. Unhealthy concentrations of nitrates are controlled by denitrifying bacteria that convert it to nitrous oxide or molecular nitrogen and by regular partial water changes.

There is then a sequence of events in this biological cycle. First of all there is a buildup of ammonia products. This is broken down into nitrites by bacteria. Following this a different set of bacteria converts the nitrites to nitrates.

Getting back to our newly set up aquarium, how do we obtain these bacteria and where do they live? First of all, they live pretty much all over the aquarium but are concentrated in the filter material (including that covering the undergravel filter), where most of their food has accumulated. They need oxygen to survive (aerobic bacteria) and receive it in the water that is constantly passing through. This is in contrast to bacteria that live in places where there is no oxygen (anaerobic bacteria), some of which are seen in aquarium substrates that have turned black and smelly. It is possible that if the filter stops operating and the oxygen becomes depleted (which it does rather quickly) the "good" bacteria will die off and be replaced by the "bad" anaerobic type. So be sure your filter is operating properly with a good flow of

Fairy Basslet (Gramma loreto).

Blackcap Basslet (Gramma melacara).

Belted Cardinalfish (Apogon townsendi).

Redspotted Hawkfish (Amblycirrhitus pinos).

water through it. In fact, a faster flow than that in a comparable freshwater tank is recommended so that it does not become stagnant.

Since the bacteria we need live in filter material, it is possible to start a culture by adding to a newly set up filter some of the material from an already established biological filter. Your aquarium store manager will probably be able to supply this. Otherwise, a few chopped clams placed in the new tank will get things started. This latter method of course will take somewhat longer as you are starting with a much smaller culture. Adding fishes to the tank will also start things going, but these fishes will have to survive the ammonia and nitrite "blooms," and there are not too many that can do this. Damselfishes are hardy fishes that have been used successfully in the past, but even some of them succumb. It is best to avoid sacrificing such fishes to get the biological filter started when the other methods described are sufficient.

But how do we know what is happening in our tank? There is certainly no really visible evidence (sometimes a clouding of the water will occur but not always) that we can actually see. Is there a particular time period that we must wait? The answer is no. We can guess how long it would take for the various cycles to occur, but there are easier and more precise

methods. You can periodically take samples of your tank water to your marine aquarium store for testing or you can do the testing for yourself with available test kits. By daily testing you can almost "see" the events that are taking place. First your water will test high in ammonia. Then, as the first bacteria build up in numbers with the availability of all that ammonia and convert the ammonia to nitrites, your water will test high in nitrites and low in ammonia. As the next set of bacteria build up with this rich new food supply and convert it to nitrates, your water will test negatively for ammonia and nitrites and higher in nitrates. These *Nitrobacter* are inhibited by the presence of ammonia, so it is only after the *Nitrosomonas* do their job

that they are able to "bloom." When the nitrogen cycle has reached the point where ammonia and nitrites are near zero, your tank should be ready to accept your first fishes.

During part of the time it takes for the biological filter to become operational, the light in the aquarium should be left on 24 hours a day to build up an algal growth.

Some aquarists are turned off by the coating of green on their beautiful, clean coral pieces, but the fishes seem to appreciate it when they are placed in the tank. Once the algal carpet is well developed the light can be reduced to about 12 hours a day.

With the biological filter in operation and the algal carpet well advanced, the tank is ready for its first fishes.

The tanks are ready when the biological filter is working properly and there is a nice algal carpet on the corals. A few fishes have already been added to these two tanks.

Fish Selection

Certainly as you travel back and forth to the aquarium store where you are purchasing your equipment and receiving advice, you are looking closely at the fishes there and mentally selecting those that you want for your tank. Unfortunately, you cannot just select those that appeal to you, bring them home, and expect them to be compatible with one another and live long and happy lives. Just as in freshwater aquaria, there are compatible species and non-compatible ones, easy to keep fishes and hard to keep fishes. You certainly do not want to purchase a beautiful but expensive fish only to put it in a tank with another fish that takes one look at it and thinks, "dinner is served." And you most assuredly do not want to select any fishes that may decide to give up the ghost after only a day or two in your tank or that will only eat a specific hard-to-get item and slowly starve before your eyes. What you want are

Study the fishes you expect to eventually purchase to see if they are healthy and active. Watch them being fed if possible and make note of how much and what they eat.

some attractive but tough customers that will thrive in your aquarium (even though you might make a small error now and again) until you really become a seasoned marine aquarist. You can search through the literature until you come up with a list of fishes that fill the bill—ones that are rugged, eat almost anything, and make little or no trouble for their tankmates—or you can seek advice from your dealer, or both.

Damselfishes are usually touted as the best fishes for beginning marine aquarists. They are. Their only drawback is their scrappy nature, but give them enough room and you will find they are admirable starters. Other good beginning fishes are batfish (*Platax orbicularis*), many groupers (be careful, as some grow very large and most are predators), anemonefishes, most gobies, and even a few butterflyfishes and pygmy angelfishes. The fishes will be discussed more thoroughly in another section of this book. Your aquarium store manager should also help you with your selection since he knows his fishes and also knows what he can get for you.

Once you have the species you want in mind, watch them carefully in the store. You can learn an awful lot about them before you actually have them in your care just by watching them at every opportunity. The more you know about them to begin with, the better

*Jewel Fish (*Microspathodon chrysurus*).

*Sunshine Damselfish (*Chromis insolatus*).

*Shy Hamlet (*Hypoplectrus guttavarius*).

*Tobacco Fish (*Serranus tabacarius*).

your chances of being able to keep them alive and well for long periods of time.

When you are ready to purchase your fishes take a good, long look at them. They should be eating well, moving about the tank properly (active if they are active species), be alert, have good coloration, show no signs of disease (spots, sores, clouded eyes, etc.), and be free of parasites (they should not be scratching themselves on the gravel or coral). Their respiration should be normal. Stressed fishes often will show that they are unhappy by breathing rapidly (shown by the gill cover movements). The fins should be relatively intact with no fungal growth on any of them. Finally, the fishes should be behaving normally. Many of these conditions can only be observed and evaluated by an experienced person, one who knows the fishes well enough to see any idiosyncrasies in their demeanor or behavior. You will get this way after having kept your fishes for a while and watching them on a day to day basis, but until then you may have to rely on the store manager. Since he wants your continued patronage he should be willing to help you make the selection. He should steer you toward some inexpensive, hardy damselfishes or even anemonefishes, although the latter usually means the purchase of an anemone to go along with them. If you can hold yourself in check and take his advice, you are on your way.

Start conservatively. Do not attempt to fill the tank with fishes immediately. Although there are some problems encountered when adding certain fishes to an established tank, it is best to try a couple of small fishes and see how they fare. After that you can add a few more from time to time as space permits. It is difficult to judge

Left: *The selection of fishes should be wide enough for anybody's taste in most dealer's shops.* **Right:** *Fishes are transported by means of plastic bags. Make sure the dealer knows how long it will be before the fishes will arrive at home so they can bag them properly.*

the holding capacity of a tank since most of the fishes have different requirements regarding space, oxygen, pollution tolerance, and so forth. Generally speaking, a marine tank can house about half the number of fishes that a freshwater tank can accommodate. Remember to allow extra room if you have selected juveniles of species that grow large as adults. Too many aquarists fill their tank to capacity(or, unfortunately, over capacity) only to find that the fish grow quickly and they are running into trouble. It is

best to select species that remain small as adults, especially if you have started with a small (less than 50 gallons) tank.

Once the fishes have been selected they will be bagged for your trip home. Always indicate to the dealer how long you expect it to be before they will be placed in their new home. If you live far from the store, perhaps they should be placed in a larger bag with some oxygen added. If it is very hot or cold outside, make sure the fishes are well insulated. Fishes that may be

perfectly healthy when they leave the store can easily catch a chill and come down with some disease if improperly handled. Large styrofoam boxes serve as great transporting containers since they are good insulators and you can keep the fishes in the dark while traveling. Keeping them in the dark usually quiets them down a bit and they tend to use less oxygen from the limited supply in the bag. Actually, the problem is that the carbon dioxide builds up rather than the oxygen is depleted. Lying the bag on its side may help as this provides the greatest surface area for the fishes.

A well aged commercial marine aquarium with healthy fishes. Note the carpet of algae on the gravel. The fishes are mostly wrasses and butterflyfishes.

Adding New Fishes to Your Aquarium

Upon arrival at your home with one or more plastic bags of new fishes there are certain steps that must be followed to properly introduce them into your aquarium. If it is a new tank that is properly aged you can start by floating the bags on the surface of the tank to equalize the temperature. The water itself will act as a buffer and the temperature will change gradually providing the temperature difference is not too great. You can also open the bags and float them in the aquarium with the open end up if you are concerned about the carbon dioxide buildup in the bags. It is also possible to add an airstone to the open bag in emergencies. Be careful that the bags don't tilt and release the fishes into the tank too early. The edges of the bag can rest on the edges of the tank (using a clothespin to hold them in place if necessary).

Two differently set up marine aquaria. Marine aquascaping is a real art and really "natural" scenes can be constructed.

Several pieces of coral can be cleaned (the white ones) for beauty leaving the algal mat on the others for the fishes' benefit.

When the temperature is approximately the same in the bag and tank you can start adding a bit of tank water to the bag. A quick pH and chemical check will indicate to you how much difference there is between the two and how careful you must be. If the bag starts to fill up with water, the excess can be dipped out and discarded. By slowly adding tank water to the bag you are acclimating the fishes to the conditions they are expected to live in. Do not be in a hurry if the fishes are not in any distress. Eventually there will be only a negligible difference between the bag and tank water and the bags can be tipped over and the fishes released. They might show some fright behavior and faded patterns for a while. After all, they have just undergone quite a traumatic experience, being netted from their old "home," bounced around in a confined plastic bag, floated in a strange tank, and finally released into it. To help the fishes adjust it might be a good idea to leave the aquarium lights off while the fishes are being acclimated. They should recover quickly and soon be swimming around in a normal manner.

There is another way to acclimate fishes, one that is used by the dealers when receiving new fishes. This is called the drip method. The fishes are received in plastic bags much like the one you will be returning home with. The dealer has previously selected the tank that each fish will be placed in and has placed a plastic container (like a kitty litter tray) on the floor in front of it. There is a length of plastic air line tubing running from the tank toward the tray and hanging directly over it, with a clamp on this tubing holding back the water from the tank. The plastic bags are opened, the contents (fishes and water) are dumped into the tray, and the clamp is opened a bit to allow water from the tank to drip into the tray. The rate of drip is regulated by how different the chemistries of the water in the bag and tank are, with a faster drip permissible when the chemistries are closer. The drip is slow when there is a great difference in order to prevent too fast a change that could possibly lead to shock and perhaps even death in the

fishes. The water chemistries should equalize before the tray is nearly full (this can be checked periodically) or some of the water can be bailed out of the tray to make room. When the waters have equalized the fishes can safely be removed from the tray and placed in the tank. There are some precautions that must be heeded with this method. Never, never leave it untended! The tray could easily overflow onto your carpet and, worse, you could siphon the whole tank out onto the floor.

Be sure that once the fishes are safely in the new tank it is properly covered. New fishes in their fright often

An anemonefish, Amphiprion *sp. peeking tentatively out from the safety of the tentacles of its anemone.*

leap out of the tank. Keep the lights off for a while. There will be plenty of time to watch them later.

Perhaps this is the time to deal with adding fishes to an aquarium that already has fishes in it. Most aquarists, I am sorry to say, throw caution to the winds and go through

An adult Pomacanthus maculosus *in its natural habitat. Juveniles of this species are similar to the Blue Koran and Emperor Angelfishes.*

the above procedures as if the tank were empty. There are two problems with this. First, you might be introducing some disease into the tank with the new fishes and thus starting an epidemic. This is minimized, of course, by your having observed them closely in your dealer's tanks, but there is always the new arrival that attracts your attention and you just cannot wait to make sure it is perfectly healthy. If possible, try to hold off buying a new addition on impulse. Perhaps the dealer will take a deposit on the fish and later, when the fish has adjusted, you can complete the transaction. Second, the new fishes might be seen as competition to the established species and be attacked or hounded to death.

The first problem is eliminated to a great extent by quarantining the fishes for a week or two before adding them to the tank. Although some quarantine tanks are bare antiseptic tanks, most experienced aquarists advocate the quarantine tank as being a miniature of the tank where they will finally be housed. The chemistry should be the same as well. This helps reduce the stress the fish will have to endure during this period. In fact, one aquarist is of the opinion that the stress caused by the quarantine is worse than the risk of contagion by placing the fishes directly into the community tank. This is up to you. During the quarantine period they should be watched carefully for any signs of diseases or parasites. The addition of some antibiotics to the quarantine water is recommended by some aquarists but frowned upon

Gobiodon citrinus *likes to hide among the coral branches and may easily be overlooked during inventory of the tank inhabitants.*

Overcrowding is more disastrous in a marine tank than a freshwater tank. Avoid it or face the consequences.

by others. Antibiotics can be obtained from your fish dealer in the form of a quarantine bath or similar solution. When you are sure that the new fishes are harboring no unwanted guests, they can be added to the main tank. If you have carefully adjusted the quarantine water chemistry and temperature to the tank chemistry and temperature (as you should), the new fishes can be moved easily and without delay.

The second problem is not so easily handled. The best way is to add only fishes that can take care of themselves. This greatly restricts, however, the types of fishes that can be added. If the tank houses strictly territorial fishes you can rearrange the

A lone soldierfish Myripristis jacobus *caught out in the open in its natural habitat. These fishes are usually very secretive.*

decor to effectively destroy the territories. The new fishes that are added are then on an almost equal footing when new territories are set up. I say almost because the older residents have the advantage of not having been moved from the pet shop before having to fight for their territories.

A more drastic method is to partition off part of the tank with a glass divider and keep the newcomers separate from the old residents until they get used to each other. When the glass divider is removed the fishes may mingle like old friends—or they may have just been waiting for this opportunity to bash each other's brains out. At least the newcomers have become acclimated to their new surroundings and are not at

such a disadvantage at this time. Again, rely on the advice given by your aquarium store's manager.

Sometimes by adding food at the time new fishes are introduced you can divert the old residents' attention at this critical time. By the time they have become full they have missed their opportunity to "welcome" the newcomers with an attack. On the other hand, some fishes become much more belligerent during feeding time and attack other fishes, chasing them out of the feeding area before they even start on the food. I suggest feeding the regular inhabitants before the new fishes are added. The contented, well-fed residents will probably be less inclined to do battle and the new fishes are perhaps too frightened to think about food.

This is actually two schools of fish, the one behind with the dark bars being Anisotremus virginicus *while the fish in the forground with the blue and yellow stripes is* Haemulon sciurus.

Even if they do feed they may wind up with the equivalent of a human's upset stomach.

When adding fishes to an established tank, take a minute to evaluate the possible reactions of the species that are involved and prepare accordingly. Be poised with a rescue net when the new ones are added, and keep an eye on things for a while before you relax and assume everything is okay. Remember, some fishes are cautious about attacking a newcomer at first, but eventually they perceive that they can win out over them and begin their delayed attack.

Foods and Feeding

Many types of fishes will eat a variety of items and pose no real feeding problems. There is now available in the pet shop an excellent selection of foods especially packaged for marine fishes, including frozen, freeze-dried, and flake foods. It is up to the aquarist to obtain an assortment of these and prepare a feeding schedule that will give his fishes a well-balanced, nutritious diet.

The addition of live foods can be made on a regular basis or according to the availability of the food. Brine shrimp in all its forms has been the mainstay of marine fish diets and probably will continue to be so for some time to come, at least until something better hits the market. Live adult brine shrimp are usually available at your dealer or you can hatch and raise your own. Several methods are discussed in the literature, and there are even brine shrimp kits available with full instructions. In the absence of live brine shrimp there are always frozen and freeze-dried packages available.

Among other packaged items available are chopped clams, chopped shrimp, chopped squid, copepods, and euphausids (krill), and algae are available for the herbivores. Of course you can

Many fishes will take advantage of an opened clam. This Chelmon rostratus *takes tiny bites out of it.*

54

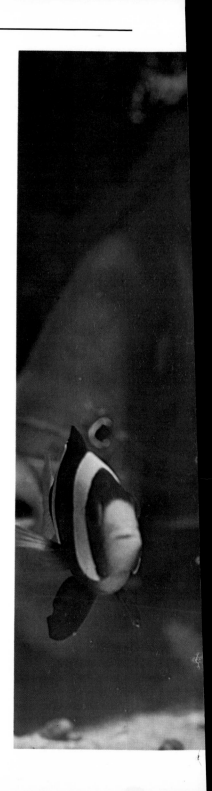

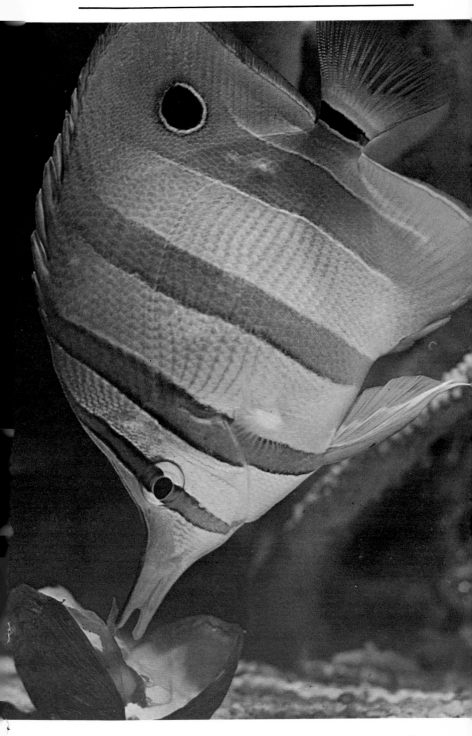

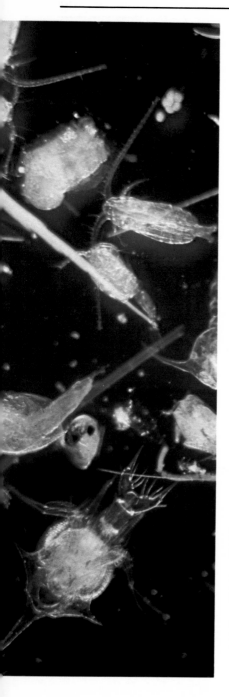

always get similar items from your local fish market or the fish counter at your supermarket, chop them up, and freeze them for future use. Some aquarists even freeze the whole animals and shave off bite-sized pieces for the fishes. Be sure that the size of the food particles fed is appropriate for the fishes involved. Small-mouthed fishes usually require small food items, although some are well able to snatch tiny bites off larger pieces of food. Large fishes need substantial pieces if they are ever going to be filled up. In other words, do not feed large groupers baby brine shrimp; they need larger chunks of food or even small live fishes such as feeder guppies or feeder goldfish.

Some foods are especially packaged for marine fishes, like this tropical plankton (below), most of which consists of copepods and crustacean larvae (left).

The mainstay of the marine fish's diet is of course all types of brine shrimp. Shown here are freeze-dried (above) and live (below) adult brine shrimp.

Then there are the fishes that have more specialized diets. Some will eat only live foods. Live brine shrimp can fill the bill for many of these, although others are more selective in what they require. Perhaps it is best for beginners not to keep these fishes, at least until they become more expert at

Some difficult butterflyfishes can be enticed to feed on coral impregnated with shrimp or other suitable food.

some may survive for a while, they eventually decline. There are also several butterflyfishes, for example *Chaetodon trifasciatus,* that feed on living corals, declining without such a diet. Although some of these can be "tricked" into feeding by placing shrimp or other goodies on dead coral, you are generally fighting a losing battle.

Among the very specialized feeders are the parasite pickers. Some part-time parasite pickers do well enough in the aquarium, for they can use other foods to supplement their diets or change over entirely to other foods. Certain species, wrasses of the genus *Labroides* for example, feed almost exclusively on parasites and waste away when they have cleaned up everything available in the tank. After all, you have specifically selected your fishes to be free of parasites and have quarantined them to get rid of unseen ones, so there should not be much left for a parasite picker to eat.

Herbivores specialize in eating green vegetable matter. This can be in the form of algae that can be grown in the tank itself (remember leaving the light on for 24 hours a day at the beginning?), in the packaged form available at your pet store, or as substitutes in the form of spinach, lettuce, zucchini, or even peas and other green vegetables. These

marine aquarium keeping. Even advanced marine hobbyists know that certain fishes cannot be maintained without a ready supply of the foods they require. If it is not available there is no way they can expect to keep that species alive. One example is always given: the natural diet of the Caribbean rock beauty *(Holacanthus tricolor)* is a certain type of orange sponge. Without it they do not do very well and, although same items can be given to fishes that are classified as omnivores—those that eat both vegetable and animal matter as a supplement to their diets.

In the store, watch the fishes you are planning on keeping and see what the manager there is feeding them. Whatever he is using should be available to you. Observe how they are fed and how much is given. You can avoid an awful lot of pitfalls by such precautions.

Feed sparingly at first, making sure every fish in the tank gets its share. Check the bottom-feeders to see that

*The Rock Beauty (*Holacanthus tricolor*) should receive a certain type of red sponge in its diet. Without it this species does not do as well as it should.*

food reaches them, although hungry bottom-feeders are not averse to swimming up toward the top of the tank in order to obtain food. Be wary of fishes that grab a piece of food and run to a hiding place. They are apt to drop it there and come back for more. The hidden food may be found and eaten later by this or other fishes, but if it is not it is a source of pollution. Although it may be easier to clean up after feeding if the fishes are fed over a particular spot, it is sometimes necessary to place food in the tank at different positions so that the more delicate or less aggressive feeders can get some. Small feedings at frequent intervals are almost always better than one large feeding per day.

Foods and Feeding

Some fishes are only able to handle a small amount at a time, and once-daily feedings are just not enough. Three to four times a day is the generally recommended schedule. You may notice that there is a difference in feeding behavior between some freshwater fishes and most marines. Whereas the freshwater fishes will eat until they nearly burst, marine fishes will often eat their fill and ignore any more food in the tank. But they are hungry again later, so food should be offered regularly to keep them in the best of shape. On the other hand, there are some marine fishes that eat a great deal at one time and are not ready to feed again for a couple of days. Your dealer can point these out to you.

Fishes feed in many different ways, and it behooves you to know how each of your charges feeds so you can supply them with the proper food in the proper manner. Many fishes will take only living foods, but others may take foods that simulate live foods—food that is moving. By placing the food in the return flow from the filter it will be "blown" across the tank, and these fishes dash after it as if it were alive. When these morsels of food eventually fall to the bottom the same fishes that avidly chase them will ignore them completely (unless you recover them and once again give them artificial motion). Some fishes must be fed by hand: the food must be placed directly in front of their noses before they deign to sample it. Forceps or their equivalent can be used if the species involved might strike at the fingers that hold the food. Certain moray eels can be fed this way with their favorite food, squids. Goatfishes search for their food on the bottom by using their barbels much like

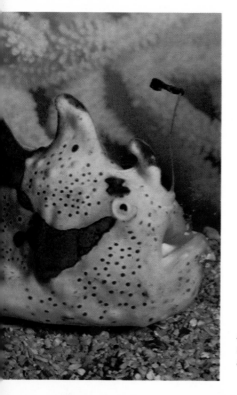

Antennariids actually "fish" for food using a spine modified into a "pole" and "bait." This is Antennarius maculatus.

60

Heniochus acuminatus *and*
Amphiprion ocellaris *are enjoying
a bunch of freeze-dried tubificid
worms.*

catfishes. Frogfishes are
unusual in that they "angle"
for their food. They have their
first dorsal fin spines modified
into a "rod" at the end of
which is a "bait," usually a
worm-like appendage. The
frogfish waves this in the
water to attract small fishes
close enough that they can
snap them up. Parrotfishes
nibble on live corals in nature
to get to the symbiotic algae
just under the coral's surface.
Some fishes have such
powerful jaws that they can
crush molluscs or
crustaceans easily. This is
something to remember if you
want to keep both fishes and
invertebrates in the same
tank. There are fishes that
have elongated snouts that
enable them to reach food
particles that have fallen into
the coral interstices out of
reach of the short-snouted
forms.

Feed according to your
fishes' needs, not according
to your fancy. This includes
the type, amount, and
schedule. If you cannot feed
them properly, do not keep
them.

Maintenance

Maintenance of a marine aquarium is very important. Many of the chores are similar to those done by a freshwater aquarist, for example the ever-necessary water changes. In a marine tank, however, water changes take on an added importance. They not only remove some of the pollutants that cannot be handled by the filtration system, but they give the marine aquarist the opportunity to get the water chemistry back into balance if it has gone awry. By this I mean that the aquarist can check his water chemistry before the water change and adjust the new water so that the chemistry will be correct when he is done. For example, there will have been some evaporation in the interval between water changes. This causes the salinity to increase because the salts do not evaporate with the water to any extent. Some salts are lost from solution, as can be seen by the encrustation on the glass cover and upper sides of the tank, but these should not affect the balance that much. (These salt marks should be cleaned off, of course.) The new water can be more diluted so that the specific gravity will be brought back to the value you want. Actually, this adjustment should not have to be too great if you have been monitoring specific gravity. If the specific gravity has been rising too fast, you can always add distilled water

to bring it back near the values desired.

If you are making regular water changes (and you should) you can have a batch of water already mixed and aged and ready for the change. Five-gallon carboys are excellent storage containers. If you mix up a batch of water just for the

A pair of Pygoplites diacanthus *frolic on the reef. Periodic water changes are necessary to keep the tank water closer to the natural reef water so that these fishes are not stressed.*

water change, you can do so easily in other temporary containers—a plastic bucket or clean plastic garbage pail (for larger amounts) will do nicely. Remove the portion of old water that you are changing, paying careful attention to filters and heaters that might become exposed or inoperative due to the lower water level. These can be unplugged for the short time necessary for the change. The new water (which should have been adjusted to the proper chemistry and temperature) can be added carefully to bring the level of the tank water to the proper position. Heaters, filters, and other accessories can then be restarted. If premixed water is not easy for you to store, the package will last for quite some time and you can mix the water a day or two before the water change. Be sure to add the proper amount of trace elements to the new water each time you make a change.

The chemistry of your aquarium water should be checked on a regular basis because the pH has a tendency to drift toward the acid side. This drift should be very slight, and regular water changes should effectively

bring it back to the desired value. If the drift happens rather quickly you must look into the reasons. These usually are overcrowding, overfeeding, or perhaps even an unnoticed dead fish in the tank. In other words, decomposition of wastes, neglected food, and dead fishes changes the pH toward the acid side, and if there is too much of this going on the tank could be going bad. Keep a close check on the pH; it is a good indication of how the tank is functioning.

Keep a periodic check on the ammonia, nitrites, and nitrates as well for the same reasons as just stated. The biological filter can handle just so much. After that capacity has been exceeded the fishes are in danger of poisoning by a buildup of

Multitest kits are useful, if not necessary, in maintaining marine aquaria. You are well ahead of the game if you know the chemistry of your sea water.

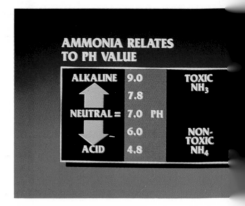

It is not usually known that the more alkaline the water the higher capacity it has for ammonia.

ammonia or nitrite. Again, overfeeding, overcrowding, and decaying food or dead fishes are the major causes. Frequent water changes help, especially if the old water is removed in combination with siphoning out of the detritus on the bottom. If you detect a rise in ammonia or nitrites, schedule an immediate water change. While doing this also check to see if there is an

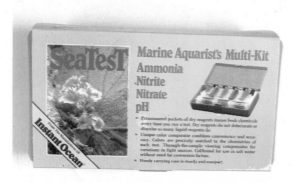

Packaged salts can be stored conveniently and ready to mix for the water changes. Make sure you read the instructions carefully so that you can plan ahead.

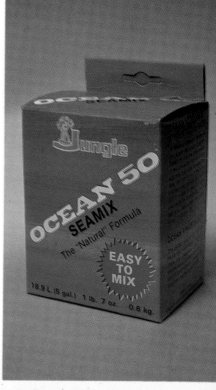

obvious reason for the unexpected rise of these substances. Removing the source and changing the water to get things back to normal are necessary procedures.

If the filter becomes clogged and needs cleaning, remember to save enough of the filter material to ensure that the biological filter will be back operating as quickly as possible. This is another reason that early marine aquarists lost some fishes.

The specific gravity can be easily checked by means of a hydrometer in the manner shown. Periodic checks are recommended.

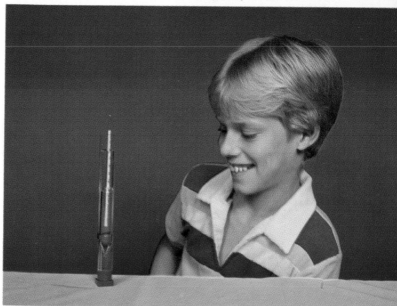

They were unaware of the biological filter and assumed that a sparkling clean filter was beneficial to their fishes. Not so. Some aquarists have a double filtering system so that one biological filter will be operating while the other is being cleaned.

The front glass can be cleaned of algal growth from time to time for better viewing of your fishes. A constant eye on the thermometer should indicate whether or not your heater is functioning properly. Airstones should be cleaned if they become clogged, and periodically the salt that accumulates from the spray of the filter, airstones, etc., should be removed.

On a daily basis you should also take a census of your fishes. Although there are hiders, you should know after a short time observing them where each individual "hangs out" and can easily discover if one is missing. This is to prevent problems if one of the fishes unexpectedly dies (unfortunately they do—often for no apparent reason). The sooner you discover the body, the fewer pollution problems you will have. If one or more fishes are found dead, make an immediate check of the chemistry and schedule a water change.

Many aquarists combine fishes with invertebrates making a much more natural looking tank. This is best left to the more advanced marine hobbyists.

Spawning Marine Fishes

A few years back it was almost unheard of to have a section of a marine aquarium book dealing with spawning or breeding marine fishes. Early marine aquarists were happy enough just to be able to keep their fishes alive, but we have entered upon a new era in marine fishkeeping, an era in which breeding marine species will become more and more common. Several species are already being produced commercially. Think of it—to be able to go into a marine aquarium store to purchase tank-raised fishes! Now that we are able to keep the species alive and happy

for considerable lengths of time, we can start to pay attention to their activities and needs as far as spawning is concerned.

There are limitations, of course. Many of the fishes kept by marine aquarists today are fairly large as adults. Some of the angelfishes, for example, grow to more than a foot in length. Imagine the size of the tanks needed to spawn some of the adult groupers!

But there are a number of smaller fishes, and also fishes that reach maturity and will spawn at sizes well below their adult sizes, available to aquarists. Foremost among these are members of two families, the damselfishes (including the anemonefishes) and the gobies. It just so happens that the first successful spawnings were from members of each of these families. The goby was the ever-popular neon goby from the Caribbean, and the anemonefish was the common clown anemonefish of the Indo-Pacific. Both are substrate spawners; that is, they select a site such as a coral branch or shell on which to lay their eggs and clean it meticulously. The eggs are

Amphiprion ocellaris is one of the first marine fishes to be spawned in commercial quantities.

A pair of Amphiprion ocellaris *spawning near their home anemone. The female is tending the eggs as the male waits in the background.*

deposited on this cleaned area by the female and fertilized by the male following close behind. In both instances the eggs are guarded by one or both parents. Once hatched, however, the fry are on their own. In the wild the newly hatched larvae exist in the water column, where they develop for a period of time determined by the species involved. After they spend their larval period in this pelagic environment they then reach a point where they are attracted back to the reef and metamorphose into recognizable juveniles. Unfortunately for aquarists, many fishes have similar life cycles but the length of life in the open waters is too long for the aquarist to have any possibility of keeping them alive.

Anemonefishes have one major factor in their favor. Most species normally prefer to deposit their eggs in the

shelter of an anemone. The stinging tentacles and the ferocity of the guarding parents combine to drive off any potential predators on the eggs. Since anemonefishes are most often kept with anemones anyway, they will probably spawn at intervals without much coaxing.

Species of the genus *Dascyllus* have also spawned in captivity. Most select branching coral (usually available to them in home aquaria) on which to deposit their eggs.

Cardinalfishes are unusual in that many are mouthbrooders. That is, the eggs are laid and fertilized on a substrate and then picked up by one of the parents in its mouth. The eggs are held there until they hatch, at which time the fry are freed into the water column. Cardinalfishes that I am familiar with will feed during the incubation period. They simply drop the egg mass, take some food, and then retrieve the egg mass again.

Seahorses and their relatives, the pipefishes, are quite unique. The female transfers the eggs to the male's special brood pouch, where they develop. When the

A pair of Tomato Clownfish (Amphiprion frenatus) spawning cichlid fashion next to the protection of their anemone. The eggs (seen as a pinkish mass on the rock) are firmly attached to the substrate.

young seahorses are ready to be born it is the male who goes through the exertions of giving birth. It is a sight to see the little miniature seahorses popping out of pappa's pouch and swimming off to find some perch around which they can wrap their tails. Be sure there is an ample supply of such perches available in the aquarium in preparation for their arrival. Even so, it is quite comical to see the little seahorses that have encountered pappa's snout and have their tails wrapped securely around it.

Frogfishes (antennariids) extrude their eggs embedded in a large gelatinous mass. This goes floating off into the open waters where the eggs eventually hatch at a later time.

Many fishes go through elaborate courtships that end with a rush toward the surface, at which time eggs and sperm are simultaneously extruded. Once released, the fertilized eggs drift off and the parents pay them no heed except to eat a few here and there. Some wrasses and parrotfishes exhibit this type of spawning.

The pattern in most marine spawnings is to

Once egg-laying has been completed, the parents stand guard over the egg mass. Most successful spawnings have been accomplished with anemones in the tank. Perhaps this gives the spawners a greater feeling of security.

release the eggs and/or fry into the open waters. This is partially to propel them into an area where there is abundant suitable food and partially to get them away from the teeming life of the reef where so many hungry animals would like some caviar for dinner. The problem for aquarists is how to treat the eggs and larvae while they are in the pelagic stage. Mostly those eggs and larvae that survive are placed in bare all-glass tanks with mild aeration. The tanks are kept scrupulously clean and selected amounts of food are introduced once the eggs have hatched and yolk sacs have been absorbed.

The main obstacle to raising the young of marine reef fishes has been the food. Newly hatched brine shrimp are excellent for many newly hatched marine fishes, but they do have their limitations. Now, however, manufacturers have started addressing this need and are developing

Above: *This Neon Goby (Gobiosoma oceanops) has chosen a PVC tube for its nest and is removing unwanted gravel from it.* **Below:** *The male Neon Goby is leading the egg-laden female into his nest in preparation for spawning.*

appropriate packaged food for marine fish larvae. Also, excellent progress has been made with culturing of a marine rotifer, *Brachionus plicatilis.*

Brachionus plicatilis is not hard to culture. Once a starter culture is obtained (some aquaculture establishments sell such cultures or perhaps your dealer can get one for you) it has to be fed single-celled algae. The algae can probably be obtained from the same source as the rotifer culture. The algae are easily cultivated with a good light source and a nutrient mix (nitrate, phosphate, and iron—much like plant fertilizers). A second method is to feed the rotifers dry activated yeast. This is best accomplished under sunlight to inhibit unwanted bacterial growth. The rotifers reproduce asexually and reach harvestable densities of up to 100 animals per milliliter in three days under optimum conditions of concentrated

Above: *Once the eggs have been deposited in the nest the male Neon Goby stands guard over them until they hatch.*
Below: *Most cardinalfishes are mouthbrooders, with the male incubating the eggs. Here a male Apogon cyanosoma is seen with a mouthful of eggs.*

Spawning Marine Fishes

Above: *A pair of* Centropyge tibicen *in the midst of courting activities. The smallness of the species might mean they can be spawned in captivity.* **Below:** *The pair rise in the water column to discharge eggs and sperm (the light colored cloud above the fishes).*

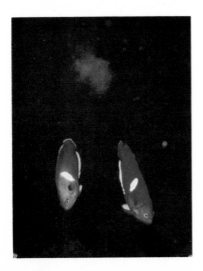

food algae at 30 parts salinity and 75°F. Additional prepared marine larval foods will undoubtedly appear at an increasing rate as demand dictates.

If you think you have a pair of a species, keep your eyes on them. Undoubtedly there have been numerous spawnings that have gone unobserved in aquarists' tanks simply because they did not watch their fishes closely enough or they did not realize what had happened. Most substrate spawners try and hide their eggs from potential predators (or prying eyes), while those fishes that scatter the eggs into the open water can usually do so safely because the eggs are virtually invisible, at least to the aquarist. In the confines of the aquarium, however, they are quickly spotted and dispatched by the other fishes in the tank (and sometimes even the spawners as well).

Once you are familiar with the general behavior of your fishes you may notice some odd goings on from time to time. This could be spawning or pre-spawning activity and should be closely watched. Perhaps you will be one of the lucky ones. If you wish to try and raise some young once the adults have spawned, you have a choice: should you leave them with the parents or hatch them separately? Usually the first batch is taken out by the aquarist and hatched separately, for the spawners are almost sure to

*A male seahorse (*Hippocampus coronatus*) giving birth to tiny replicas of itself. The young swim immediately but wrap their tails around the first appropriate object they come in contact with.*

have a repeat performance and there then will be a chance to see how well the fish tend their own eggs. It may be best, however, to skip the first batch if you were not ready for it. You can set up a rotifer culture or have some prepared food ready before the next one. Since there are more and more books and articles appearing giving details regarding marine fish spawnings, you can probably read up on the fishes you are keeping and know what to expect. Perhaps there even will be hints on how to induce them to spawn if they are somewhat reluctant.

So keep an eye on your fishes and maybe you will be the one writing about a "first" in marine fish spawning that has happened in your own tank.

Diseases And Stress

"An ounce of prevention is worth a pound of cure." How well that fits the marine aquarium situation. Many of the problems that occur in a marine (or freshwater) aquarium could have been avoided if the preventive measures available to the aquarist were taken. Looking back on the situation once disease has struck a tank, the aquarist thinks, "Would this have happened if I hadn't skipped that water change?" or "Were the last few fishes I placed in the tank just too many?" or "Why didn't I test the chemistry of the water as often as I should have?" In other words, could the situation have been prevented by following good aquarium practices? The answer in most cases is—yes.

What has poor aquarium practices to do with a disease striking aquarium fishes? Simply stated, it places stress on the fishes. A stressed fish is open to all kinds of problems just as a human who catches a chill is more likely to catch cold than one who has bundled up and kept warm. There are so many ways in which an aquarium fish can be stressed. The pH could be too acid or too alkaline (did you know that ammonia is more toxic at higher pH values?); the salinity could be too high or too low; the thermostat could be malfunctioning, causing fluctuations in the

*A Sailfin Tang (*Zebrasoma desjardinii*) with a bad case of lateral line disease.*

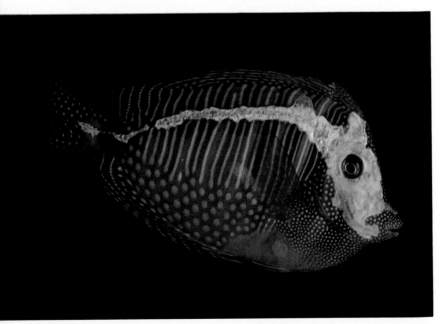

When a fish suddenly dies of no apparent reason some aquarists are able to perform an autopsy of sorts to try and find out the cause.

A quality microscope is too expensive for most aquarists and is not a necessity. If you have access to one through your aquarium society or school, use it to your advantage.

Being an inquisitive aquarist, Karen Mason wants to know why her parrotfish died unexpectedly. Genuine biological curiosity gives her the determination to conduct a necropsy.

There is no evidence of disease here. These gills appear normal, with no loss of color (a sign of anemia) and no visible parasites.

Karen discovers some internal lesions and asks for my opinion. Since most aquarists don't have a fish pathologist in the neighborhood, diseased tissues can be preserved and mailed to a lab.

Close-up photography is an excellent way to record lesions and obtain professional opinions. Dr. Axelrod photographed this diseased liver so that you could see the cysts caused by a microsporidian parasite.

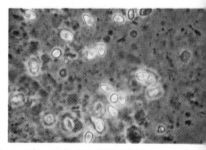

Microscopic examination of the cysts revealed numerous microsporidia. Although not the primary cause of death in this fish, all pathological changes are significant and should be recorded.

temperature or making the temperature too high or too low; the biological filter could be malfunctioning, allowing buildup of ammonia or nitrites; overfeeding; overcrowding—just to name a few. All of these factors can be controlled by the aquarist and therefore could have been prevented. Let this be a word to the wise.

If a problem develops, it is best to be able to recognize it as early as possible. It is a bit late when one or more fishes lie dead on the bottom of the tank. The fishes actually tell you that they are under stress in many ways. You just have to be observant enough and knowledgeable enough to "read" this language and act upon it. A change of color should attract your attention. When one or more of your fishes start to fade or darken, take heed—it probably means that there is trouble in the tank. I say probably because fishes do change colors for reasons other than stress. For example, spawning fishes often change color, as do some aggressive ones at times. But these color changes usually have enhanced colors and the activity of the fishes increases: they look fine. A stressed fish will often act listless, hide in a corner, and refuse food, all additional stress reactions. Rapid breathing, abnormal swimming (including "scratching" on a piece of coral or the bottom), and folded fins are also symptomatic. These early signs should start the aquarist checking all facets of the aquarium to see if

When one or more of your fishes suddenly loses color it could mean trouble brewing. A chemistry check and possibly a water change are indicated.

Color changes can tell the aquarist a great deal about the fish's health and temperament. This Chaetodon trifascialis *is shown in its normal color (above) and in a pattern that could mean sickness, fright, or simply sleeping (below).*

anything is amiss. If it is and it is easily correctable, it should be done without delay. A water change may be just the thing. More often than not, by correcting the situation the stress is removed and the day is saved. The fishes return to normal, and you should be thankful that you caught the problem in time.

It is generally accepted now that disease organisms are present in the tank and on the fishes at all times. Healthy fishes are able to counteract the effects of these organisms, so no disease is able to gain the upper hand. But when a fish is under stress its resistance is lowered and the disease organisms start to take over. Removing the stressful situation gives the fish a chance to again fight off the disease organisms and perhaps regain full health.

Once a disease organism really gets going, further symptoms may develop. The most common are: small white, gray, or yellow spots on the body or fins; cloudy eyes; one or both eyes bulging; gill covers extended and/or gills pale; open sores on body and fins; bloody areas, especially at the bases of the fins; ragged fins with cloudy edges; cottony white growths on body or fins; and cauliflower-like growths on fins. The following is a list of the most commonly encountered marine fish diseases, parasites, and other problems, their symptoms, and their cures.

SALTWATER ICH OR WHITE SPOT DISEASE

Saltwater ich is manifested in a fish by the appearance of numerous white or grayish spots on the body and fins. These spots are larger in size than those seen in marine velvet disease and do not give the fish the powdery appearance of that disease. As the disease advances, scratching on the bottom or coral decorations occurs, breathing becomes more difficult (when the gills are affected), the color becomes patchy (due partially to the color of the fish and partially to the proliferation of the disease organism), eyes become cloudy, and hemorrhaging occurs. If left untreated, the fish will die.

The cause of this disease is a ciliated protozoan parasite called *Cryptocaryon irritans*. It is generally difficult to eradicate from the aquarium, but there are several

Among the more effective treatments of common marine aquarium fish diseases are copper, formalin, and malachite green. These are packaged specifically for treating aquarium fishes.

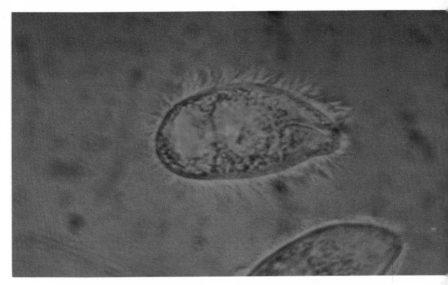

Cryptocaryon irritans, *the cause of saltwater ich. This is the free-swimming swarmer stage that can spread the disease throughout the tank.*

commercial preparations that are reasonably effective. The basic ingredients usually are either copper, formalin, or malachite green (less effective); an antimalarial drug called Quinacrine has been reported to be effective. Invertebrates should be removed from the tank when any medication containing copper is used. In fact, it is usually best to remove invertebrates before adding *any* medications to the aquarium.

VELVET OR CORAL FISH DISEASE

Velvet usually starts in the gill area, and the fish can be seen to have difficulty breathing. As the infestation progresses, scratching occurs and

eventually small white spots appear. These are quite small and can best be seen in the initial stages on clear fin membranes. Eventually the

Treatment of velvet disease usually involves copper in one form or another. Be sure to follow dosage instructions carefully.

body is covered with these spots, giving it a dusty or velvety look (hence the name). Breathing difficulty increases, and eventually the fish can be seen lying on its side on the bottom, where it soon dies.

The cause of this disease is a parasitic dinoflagellate (a type of alga) called *Oodinium ocellatum.* It has a complex life cycle with one of the stages attacking the fishes.

Oodinium ocellatum is the causative agent of velvet disease. It is a parasitic dinoflagellate. These were found on the gills of an Amphiprion ocellaris.

Nitrofurazone derivitives are used for several marine fish diseases, including vibriosis or vibrio disease.

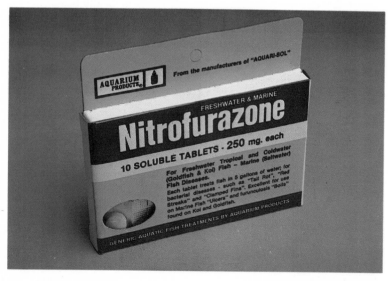

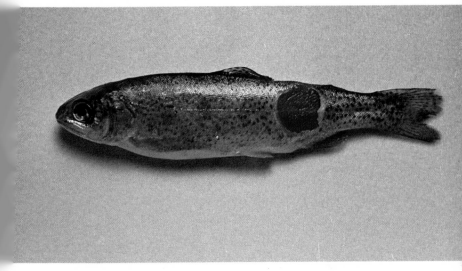

Commercial treatments are available at pet shops and usually involve copper. Freshwater baths often are successful for treating the fish, but the tank also is usually infested and it takes a chemical bath to eradicate the disease organism.

*An external lesion of vibrio disease (*Vibrio anguillarum) *in a rainbow trout.*

VIBRIOSIS OR VIBRIO DISEASE

Fishes that show a loss of appetite, listlessness, and a general darkening of the skin may have this disease. In later stages hemorrhages appear that eventually may develop into ulcerated sores. Damage also is done to the liver, kidney, and spleen. Eventually death occurs.

This disease is caused by bacteria of the genus *Vibrio* and is often associated with environmental stress.

Treatment involves improved environmental conditions and use of Furanace. Nitrofurazone derivatives can be obtained from your dealer.

FIN ROT

This problem is manifested by the deterioration of the fins, giving them ragged edges that are milky or cloudy. Eventually the whole fin could be lost, causing difficulty in swimming.

Bacterial organisms of the genera *Pseudomonas,* *Aeromonas,* and *Vibrio* are all suspected of causing fin rot. It has also been reported that lack of a particular amino acid (lysine) may be a related cause.

Improvement of environmental conditions and treatment with nitrofurazone derivatives will combat this disease.

GILL PARASITES

Fishes that keep their mouth open and exhibit pale gills rather than normal red coloration may have gill parasites, usually the fluke *Gyrodactylus.*

Freshwater or formalin baths or copper treatments usually relieve the situation.

commonly are infected by bacteria.

Freshwater baths are easiest on the fishes affected. Copper treatments may also be used.

GAS-BUBBLE DISEASE OR EXOPHTHALMOS (POP-EYE)

LYMPHOCYSTIS OR CAULIFLOWER DISEASE

The fish exhibits grayish or whitish cauliflower-like growths on its lips and/or fins. These may spread over the body but should disappear spontaneously with time.

FLUKES

These parasites usually affect the gills, skin, nasal cavities, and eyes, where they feed on the blood and mucus of their host. Scratching is evident, eventually leading to loss of scales and open wounds that

Lymphocystis or cauliflower disease in a triggerfish (Sufflamen bursa). This diseased individual was photographed in its natural habitat.

This disease is characterized by gas bubbles appearing beneath the skin and eye membranes. It generally is not biological in origin but is caused by a physical problem, excess dissolved gas (usually nitrogen) in the water. Correction of the problem causing the supersaturation of the water usually eases the problem in the fishes.

Space does not permit the full description of all diseases, their symptoms, and their cures. What appears above is just the tip of the iceberg, and for more detailed accounts I recommend you obtain a book dedicated to the diseases of fishes, of which there are many on the market. Full details of the treatments can be had in such books. Complete instructions also are given with the

A case of exophthalmus in a Copperband Butterflyfish (Chelmon rostratus). *The right eye is obviously more affected than the left.*

commercially packaged treatments at your dealers. Most of the diseases commonly encountered by marine aquarists have been thoroughly researched, and small bottles of the most effective remedy are available at the pet shop.

Invertebrates

Although the vast majority of marine aquarists deal with fishes exclusively (though some keep anemones because they want to keep anemonefishes), some aquarists are so fascinated by invertebrates that they will keep nothing else. They may have a good point. After all, there are so many different types of invertebrates available that an aquarist simply cannot exhaust the possibilities in his or her lifetime. Just think: anemones, starfishes, crabs, shrimp, corals, fanworms, squids, octopuses, gastropods, and bivalves are just a few of the groups that can be kept. Not only are they fascinating in their appearance and behavior, but some are among the most colorful of Nature's creatures.

With such a myriad of animals to choose from, generalities are difficult. The tank is set up as directed for the fishes. Care must be exercised, however, when selecting your filter material. Activated carbon should be avoided as it may deplete the water of necessary trace elements that a particular invertebrate needs. Feeding may be difficult as some invertebrates are filter-feeders and need tiny animal life drifting in the water to sustain them.

The fishes seem almost incidental in this aquarium heavily populated with invertebrates.

SEA ANEMONES AND THEIR RELATIVES

Sea anemones are of course sought after by both fish and invertebrate enthusiasts because of the symbiotic relationship between the anemonefishes and the sea anemones. They are relatively easy to keep and feed. Bringing home an anemone can be rewarding—as you put it into your tank in the form of an almost shapeless mass (it contracts when touched) and watch it expand and unfold into a beautiful flower-like animal. Anemones have stinging cells that can kill soft-bodied animals as well as fishes, so their tankmates must be chosen with care. Feeding is easily accomplished by dropping food onto the oral disc or even onto the tentacles.

Corals are almost always seen in marine tanks as bleached skeletons, but some

Above: *A colorful* Corynactis californica *from Monterey Bay.*
Left: *A Japanese anemone,* Anthopleura midori.

aquarists have been able to maintain some species alive. Feeding is usually by eyedropper for the large-polyped species and by drifting fine food in a current for smaller ones.

Sea pens and gorgonians are only occasionally maintained. They are fed much like corals.

WORMS

Worms in general do not sound like good candidates for invertebrate tanks, but once you have seen the featherduster worms you will certainly change your mind. Many of these are quite beautiful, with elaborate plumes. Feeding again takes a little patience as they must be fed small food items in a current. Newly hatched brine shrimp in the outflow of a filter have been used successfully, although some aquarists prefer a more direct method, using an eyedropper.

Flatworms sometimes come in gorgeous colors and patterns but are difficult to keep and do not last long.

MOLLUSCS

Gastropods such as cowries are often selected for invertebrate aquaria. They may crawl around the tank on their flattened foot looking for food, often algae. Some are browsers while others (such as cones) are predators, cones hunting their prey with poison darts.

Bivalves are more difficult to handle as they are almost

Colorful sabellid worms poking out from their live coral base. This combination is often sold as "living rock."

all filter-feeders. They are basically stationary and must have a current of water bring food to them. The most popular bivalve is *Lima scabra*, a scallop with a fiery red to red-orange mantle that is fringed on its edge. It also has the ability to move rather quickly by using a clapping action of its two valves.

Nudibranchs are popular because of their colors. They

*Live molluscs like this Chinese Cowry (*Cypraea chinensis*) are sometimes kept. Many are browsers and difficult to feed.*

Lima scabra is prized for its bright red mantle. It can also move quite rapidly using a form of jet propulsion.

are essentially naked snails,
lacking an external shell like
the more typical gastropods.
Unfortunately, most have
specific dietary needs that are
hard to meet and few live very
long in captivity.

Squids and octopuses are
molluscs. Some small squids
and cuttlefishes are kept, but
usually these animals are too
nervous to live very long in
captivity. Octopuses, on the
other hand, are more
sedentary and do well in
aquaria. They are quite
intelligent and are adept at
finding very small openings in
the aquarium cover when they
decide to "go for a walk."
They usually are contented
with feeding on crustaceans
(many octopuses love to eat
the fiddler crabs that can be
purchased from bait stores
along the coast).

CRUSTACEANS
Perhaps it is this group that
contributes the most animals
to marine invertebrate
aquaria. These include crabs,
shrimp, lobsters, barnacles,
and hermit crabs, to name
just a few.

Cleaner shrimp are often
kept. They are called cleaners
because they actually remove
(and eat) parasites from the
fishes that present
themselves in front of the

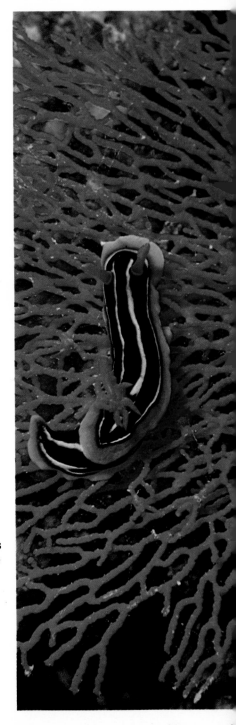

*Nudibranchs often have specific
dietary needs and may not last
long. They are often brightly
colored and most aquarists are
willing to try them. Shown is
Glossodoris sp.*

91

cleaning "station." The best known cleaning shrimp is *Stenopus hispidus*, the candy cane shrimp, so called because of its red and white banded pattern. Other cleaners of the genera

Above: Stenopus hispidus *is a cleaner shrimp regularly kept by invertebrate enthusiasts.* **Below:** *Hermit crabs need a variety of empty shells in the tank to occupy as they grow in size. Otherwise they fight for the few available to them. This is* Dardanus *sp.*

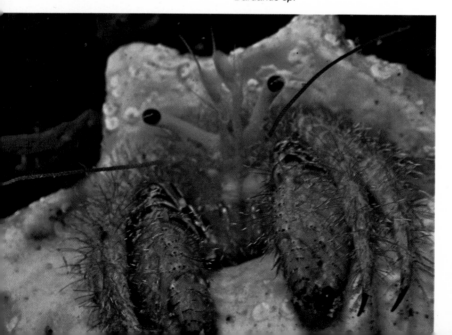

Periclimenes and *Lysmata* are gaining in popularity and may soon rival *Stenopus.*

Hermit crabs are quaint creatures that would be quite vulnerable to predators except for one thing: they truck their delicate posterior ends into an empty snail shell and drag it along with them. When frightened they simply

faced crabs of the genus *Calappa.*

STARFISHES AND THEIR RELATIVES

Starfishes come in assorted shapes and colors and have attained a limited popularity with invertebrate specialists. Some are excellent burrowers, to the

One of the shame-faced crabs, Calappa lophos. *Their large claws make them appear as if they are hiding their faces, hence the common name.*

pull back into the shell until only their claws are visible to guard the entrance. As they grow they must seek out larger shells, so if you are keeping some be sure to provide additional "housing" for them.

Several crabs and crab allies are very popular with aquarists. Porcelain crabs of the genus *Petrolisthes* sell briskly, as do the shame-

consternation of aquarists; others like to wander about the aquarium by using their tube feet for locomotion. Dead seafood forms the major portion of their diet. Brittlestars feed on small

animals and detritus.
Basketstars, large, specialized brittlestars, actively capture small animals that swim past at night by using their numerous delicate arms.

Sea urchins are sometimes kept, even the long-spined poisonous species of the genus *Diadema.* Unfortunately, when these die they usually drop their spines and create a veritable mess.

A couple of sea cucumber are kept. These are mostly detritus-feeders and pick up their food from the bottom, although the brightly red-striped ones may be filter-feeders.

There are many, many more invertebrates that appear for sale at marine aquarium shops. On each visit you will probably see something different. However, before you decide to add it to your invertebrate tank (and especially before you add it to your fish tank) find out from the dealer any problems with feeding it and its compatibility with other species.

A diademid sea urchin. Sea urchins are browsers and often difficult to feed. They will show their displeasure at times by shedding their spines and eventually dying.

Starfishes come in many different colors. This bright purple Linckia *is found in very shallow water.*

appealing you want to take home as many different kinds as possible. But you must be strong and fight down these impulses, opting instead for the species that you have the best chance of keeping alive—at least until you are experienced enough to try some of the more delicate species.

The following is a brief survey of some of the fishes available and what to expect from them.

DAMSELFISHES

These are small, colorful fishes that usually live in reefy areas where they stake out territories. Spawning individuals guard these territories, and when eggs are present even a human diver may be attacked in the fish's attempt to chase him away. They are tough, feisty critters that are well suited to aquarium life. These fishes are recommended for the beginner.

Top: *Young* Dascyllus trimaculatus *among the tentacles of an anemone. So it is not only clownfishes that seek such protection.* Dascyllus *species, however, seem to prefer live corals to anemones.* **Right:** *Many damselfishes change color and pattern considerably with growth, usually for the worse. Juveniles, like this* Paraglyphidodon bonang, *are better to start with, anyway.*

Selecting from the vast array of different fishes is probably one of the most difficult jobs facing a novice marine aquarist. They all look so

Top: *The Jewelfish (*Microspathodon chrysurus*) prefers clear, clean areas of the reef and usually can be found among stinging coral.* **Middle:** *The Beau Gregory (*Stegastes leucostictus*) is colorful, active, hardy, and a good feeder, so it is one of the beginner's favorites. It is also quarrelsome so tankmates should be chosen with care.* **Bottom:** *The Green Damselfish (*Chromis caerulea*) is another popular beginner's fish. Large aggregations of them are commonly seen on a reef.*

ANEMONEFISHES

Although technically members of the family Pomacentridae (like the damselfishes), these fishes form a group all their own. Most, if not all, species are good aquarium inhabitants. *Amphiprion*

One of the striped anemonefishes is Amphiprion clarkii. *This pair has spawned and one of the parents is tending to the cleaning and aeration of the eggs.*

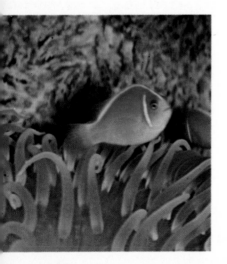

ocellaris commonly spawns in captivity and is currently being bred on a commercial basis. These fishes do best if kept with an anemone with which they maintain a commensal relationship.

Amphiprion perideraion *is one of the "skunk" anemonefishes because of the white stripe that extends along its back. Two other species,* A. sandaracinos *and* A. akallopisos *are similarly patterned but lack the white stripe across the operculum.*

A trio of Clownfish, Amphiprion ocellaris. *It is unusual to see them in a tank without immediate access to an anemone. However, they seem to do fairly well without one. The blue fish is the Blue Devil,* Glyphidodontops cyaneus.

This is basically an invertebrate aquarium, but the inclusion of the anemone has prompted the aquarist to add an anemonefish to the tank as well. It is necessary to know your fishes and invertebrates well before combining them or disaster may result for either the fishes or invertebrates — or both.

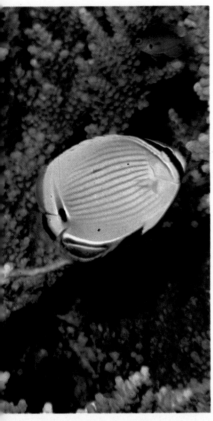

Chaetodon trifasciatus is one of the hardiest butterflyfishes to keep. It feeds on living corals (as can be seen here in its natural habitat), a diet that is not easy to provide in captivity.

BUTTERFLYFISHES

Butterflyfishes are colorful reef fishes of moderate size (to over a foot in length), some of which do well in aquaria, some not. Most of those that do not do well decline because of lack of proper food. *Chaetodon*

Heniochus acuminatus has several common names. One is the Pennant Butterflyfish because of the elongated dorsal fin spine; another is the "Poor Man's Moorish Idol" because of the lesser cost and the vague resemblance of the patterns.

Top: Chaetodon auriga *is one of the hardier butterflyfishes and seems to do reasonably well in captivity. The extended dorsal fin ray has prompted the name Threadfin Butterflyfish.* **Middle:** *One of the Caribbean favorites is the Four-eyed Butterflyfish (*Chaetodon capistratus*), the posterior spots being the extra "eyes".* **Bottom:** *The Long-snouted Butterflyfish (*Forcipiger flavissimus*) does well in captivity. Because of the elongated snout it can retrieve food items that have fallen into crevices out of the reach of short-snouted species.*

trifasciatus, for example, feeds on living coral almost exclusively. *Chaetodon auriga* and *C. lunula* do better and may be added to your tank.

*This bright yellow pygmy angelfish (*Centropyge flavissimus*) is called the Lemonpeel because of its color. The contrasting blue edging to fins and gill cover and encircling the eye distinguish this species from the related* Centropyge heraldi *.*

ANGELFISHES

Angelfishes are reef fishes that are prized aquarium fishes. Most do well, but there are several that are quite hard to keep. *Centropyge bicolor* is one of them. The pygmy angelfishes of genus *Centropyge* are generally small, while species of the genus *Pomacanthus* grow to over a foot in length. Even so, juvenile *Pomacanthus* are so colorful they are often members of a marine community tank.

*The young Blue Angelfish (*Holacanthus isabelita*) has the second white line on the body straight whereas that of the Queen Angel (not shown) is curved.*

Perhaps the favorite angelfishes from the Indo-Pacific are these two. They are both juveniles, the upper one being an Emperor Angelfish (Pomacanthus imperator), the lower photo of a Blue Koran Angelfish (Pomacanthus semicirculatus). Both species grow fairly large and change color and pattern as they do.

BATFISHES

Three species of batfishes are commonly imported for marine aquaria. One is quite easy to keep *(Platax orbicularis)*, one medium *(Platax teira)*, and one fairly difficult *(Platax pinnatus)*. You can almost trace your progress in marine fishkeeping by your ability to keep these three species alive.

The most colorful but least hardy batfish is this Platax pinnatus. *The orange edging is distinctive during the younger stages.*

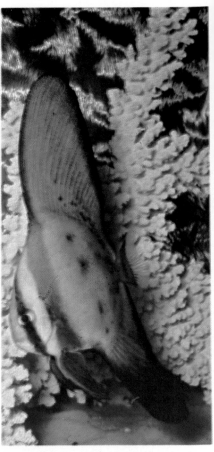

The easiest to keep but the least colorful is Platax orbicularis. *It eats well and grows very quickly, usually meaning it has to be moved to larger quarters every so often. Some individuals become quite tame and will even eat out of the owner's hand.*

Platax teira *is the one in the middle. It is not seen as often as the other two but sells well when it is available. It falls in between the other two species in both attractiveness and hardiness.*

Young Zebrasoma, *such as this* Z. veliferum, *are very appealing to aquarists. They should receive some vegetable matter in their diets.*

SURGEONFISHES

Surgeonfishes or tangs are a mixed lot. Some do very well in aquaria, some do not. Among the favorites are the powder-blue tang and several members of the genus *Zebrasoma.* Vegetable matter should be included in their diet. Be careful of the small, sharp, knife-like spines at the base of the tail of some of the species.

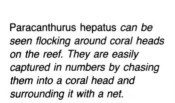

Paracanthurus hepatus *can be seen flocking around coral heads on the reef. They are easily captured in numbers by chasing them into a coral head and surrounding it with a net.*

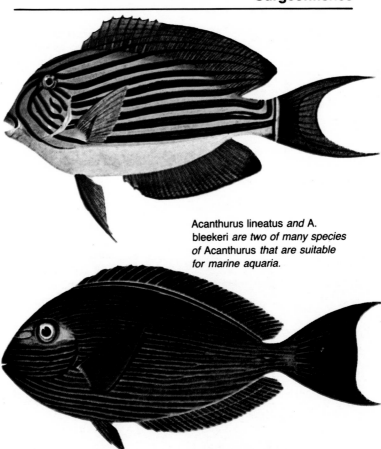

Acanthurus lineatus *and* A. bleekeri *are two of many species of* Acanthurus *that are suitable for marine aquaria.*

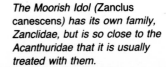

*The Moorish Idol (*Zanclus canescens*) has its own family, Zanclidae, but is so close to the Acanthuridae that it is usually treated with them.*

107

WRASSES

This is a large, very varied group of fishes, some of which do well in captivity, some not. It is best to check with your dealer as to which is which before you buy. The cleaner wrasses of the genus *Labroides* belong to this family.

Below: *The Spanish Hogfish (*Bodianus rufus*) in a very belligerent stance with its mouth open and ready for action.*

Above: *A Cleaner Wrasse* (Labroides dimidiatus) *searching a Flame Angelfish (*Centropyge loriculus*) for parasites or other edibles.*

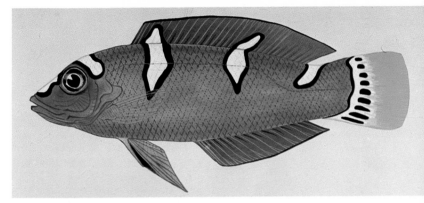

The Clown Wrasse (Coris gaimard) is one of the wrasses that will occasionally dive into the sand and disappear for a while. This causes many problems for aquarists, especially when trying to inventory the fishes.

Below: The Yellowcheek Wrasse (Halichoeres cyanocephalus) is a deeper water fish, inhabiting depths of 90 to 300 feet. Yet juveniles, as the one shown, sometimes make their way into the aquarium trade.

SCORPIONFISHES

Although some dangerous fishes belong to this family, only one group seems to regularly be found in aquarist's tanks. These are the lionfishes or turkeyfishes. As a group they do quite well and soon become quite tame. But don't become too friendly with your lionfish, for it has poisonous spines that can give you many hours of pain if you get stuck. (The antidote is immersing the stung finger in hot—*not scalding*—water until the pain stops.)

Left: *Many scorpaenids have quite a bit of ornamentation, especially in the head area. This is* Scorpaena picta. **Below:** *The Hawaiian Lionfish (*Pterois sphex). *This species is not seen as often as some of the other lionfishes.*

The two most popular lionfishes or turkeyfishes are Pterois volitans *(above) and* P. lunulata *(right). They are similar in appearance and have at times been considered a single species.* P. lunulata *generally lacks the "tentacles" above the eye. Both species can give a pretty nasty sting, somewhat worse than some of the other species, so handle with care.*

111

GROUPERS

There are a great many groupers, many of which do well in captivity but grow to enormous sizes and soon must be moved to larger quarters. Fortunately, there are some grouper relatives, the dottybacks and basslets, that remain small, are colorful, and do reasonably well in home aquaria. Most groupers are carnivores and easy to feed.

Right: *The dottybacks (members of the genus* Pseudochromis) *do well in captivity and are usually brightly colored. They should have some shelter where they can hide in an aquarium. This is* P. paccagnellae. **Below:** *Anthiids have always been well received by marine aquarists. This* Anthias pleurotaenia *has recently become one of the favorites. This individual is being cleaned by a species of* Labroides.

This Caribbean Royal Gramma (Gramma loreto) has a similar pattern to the Indo-Pacific dottyback on the opposite page but is different enough otherwise to be placed in a different genus.

Top: The Indigo Hamlet (Hypoplectrus indigo) is an uncommon species that attains a length of only about 5.5 inches. **Bottom:** The Harlequin Bass (Serranus tigrinus) rarely exceeds 4 inches and does well in captivity.

113

SEAHORSES

Seahorses are favorites of marine aquarists. They usually have to be kept by themselves because of their timidity. They are so slow in feeding that they cannot compete with most fishes. Baby guppies and live brine shrimp are favorite foods. Males give birth to the young, which are tiny replicas of their parents.

Right: *This relatively rare seahorse (*Hippocampus bargibanti*) is well disguised in its natural habitat. Perhaps some day it will be available to marine aquarists.* **Below:** Hippocampus kuda *from the West Pacific is more commonly available.*

The common seahorse from the
Western Atlantic is this
Hippocampus erectus. *This male
is giving birth to young which can
be seen hanging on to the same
gorgonid skeleton that he has his
tail wrapped around.*

*The pipefishes are in the same
family as the seahorses. This
pipefish is* Doryrhamphus
dactyliophorus, *a very colorful
species.*

115

CARDINALFISHES

These are small, usually nocturnal, and usually red in color. They do well in captivity but need some shelter from bright lights during the day. Most are mouthbrooders.

Above: Apogon maculatus *is commonly shipped from Florida.* **Left:** *A group of* Apogon cyanosoma *sheltering among the spines of diademid sea urchins. Many fishes use the urchin spines for protection, especially young ones.* **Below:** *A young* Cheilodipterus *sp.*

The Pajama Cardinalfish
(Sphaeramia nematoptera) is
preferred by marine aquarists
because it is not nocturnal and
stays out in the open where it can
be seen.

Above: A Barred Cardinalfish
(Apogon binotatus). **Below:** A
group of Sawcheek Cardinalfish
(Apogon quadrisquamatus)
among the tentacles of an
anemone.

TRIGGERFISHES AND THEIR RELATIVES

No survey can be complete without mention of the "king" of the aquarium field, the clown trigger. It is still quite expensive but usually hardy and lives a long time.

Relatives of the triggerfishes include the puffers, which usually are fin-nippers; boxfishes, which can exude a poisonous slime when upset; and spiny puffers, which like the true puffers can swallow water (or air) and swell up into a virtual balloon.

Right: Oxymonacanthus longirostris *will seek refuge in coral branches when frightened. Wedged into the coral like this it is almost impossible to remove.*

Many species of Rhinecanthus *are in the aquarium trade. They are all distinctively marked and easily identified. This one is* R. aculeatus.

The Clown Triggerfish is by far the most sought after species of triggerfish. It always commands a premium price and always seems to find a buyer. When small specimens were imported the marine aquarists literally jumped for joy.

This Hawaiian filefish is Pervagor aspricaudus. It apparently is a different species from the Indo-Pacific P. spilosoma.

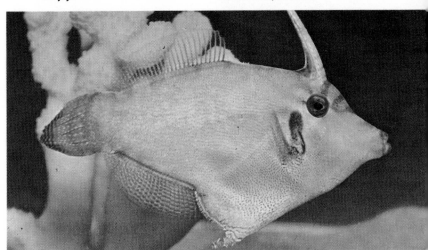

Above: Diodon hystrix *in its non-inflated aspect. When frightened it swallows water (or air if out of the water) and swells up into a ball. The spines then stick out producing a pin-cushion effect.*

Below: *A well-marked species of sharp-nosed puffer is this* Canthigaster coronata. *Almost any species of* Canthigaster *is suitable for aquaria. One problem, however, is that sharp-nosed puffers tend to be very nippy and their tankmates should be selected with this in mind.*

Upper photo: *The Spotted Trunkfish* (Lactophrys bicaudalis) *occasionally shows up for sale in aquarium shops. It comes from the tropical Western Atlantic.*
Lower photo: *More commonly available is this Scrawled Cowfish* (Acanthostracion quadricornis). *The "horns" above the eyes and the blue scrawl marks seem to make it much more appealing to aquarists.*

Right: *A young spotted trunkfish (Ostracion cubicus). The comical antics of these small fishes are perhaps their greatest appeal.*

Miscellaneous Fishes

There are numerous other families of keepable fishes that room does not permit me to discuss. There are the gobies, blennies, squirrelfishes, eels, and hawkfishes, just to name a few. A specialized book on marine fishes will give you the pertinent information needed about disposition, food requirements, size attained, and other important points.

Several blennies are commonly seen in marine aquarists' tanks. This colorful little one is Ecsenius bicolor.

Goatfishes make nice pets as well. They are almost like marine catfishes as they scour the bottom with their barbels looking for food. This is Parupeneus barberinoides.

Hawkfishes do very well in captivity. *This is* Cirrhitops fasciatus *perched among some live corals.*

Among the unusual families represented in the marine hobby is the croaker or drum family *(Sciaenidae). However, this* Equetus punctatus *(as well as its close relatives) is always welcome.*

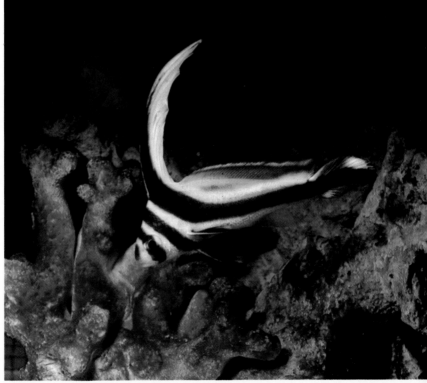

Index

One of the more popular species of Dascyllus *from the Red Sea area is this* D. marginatus.